UNSUPPORTED

A STORY OF MOVING FAST AND LETTING GO – SETTING A SPEED RECORD IN THE ADIRONDACK MOUNTAINS

BETHANY ADAMS

To all those who have found peace and love in wild places.
And for those still trying to find it.
To all touched by suicide.
For my dear cousin Chad.

Contents

June 2009

THE FORESTED PEAKS and whiskey-colored waters of the Adirondack Mountains have captured my heart. After four years of environmental studies at Paul Smith's College, I can't bear to leave. Though I miss the farmland of my central New York roots, something about this vast, jagged landscape feels like home to me. The sheer rock faces that rise to the sky, the thick pine forests, the blue ridgelines stretching toward Canada and Vermont. Plus I love the idea of being close to Lake Placid, where Olympic athletes train.

But living here isn't easy. The recession leaves my dozen job applications unanswered, so I piece together three seasonal tourism gigs just to afford the expensive vacation-destination rent. To save money, I bike and walk as much as possible, eating peanut butter and jelly sandwiches and picking wild strawberries along the roads and railroad tracks.

One day, my college friend Maegen invites me to hike Mount Marcy. I don't know much about the Adirondack High Peaks, as New York's tallest mountains are known, other than there are forty-six of them and Mount Marcy is the highest. In all my years as a student, I had been too busy playing soccer and basketball to get out and explore them, even though I could see a few from campus and most of their trailheads were less than an hour drive away. Knowing that my restless legs need a new sport, I agree to the fifteen-mile adventure.

On the day Maegen and I set out to climb Mount Marcy, rain spits from a steely sky and the parking lot of the Adirondack Loj, where the hike begins, is nearly empty. I wear a pair of black soccer shorts and a green fleece, two sizes too small, that I'd picked up at a local thrift store for three dollars and tie back my short blonde hair with a bandana I recently bought at a Bruce Springsteen concert. From the trunk of my car, I pull out an old Adidas backpack and toss a liter of water, a few Clif bars, an apple, a disposable camera, and a pair of gloves inside.

Meagan and I follow a rocky trail which snakes beside the river through balsam and birch forest. We talk about college and reminisce about ex-boyfriends until the terrain becomes steep and challenging. Eventually, the trees give way until all that's left is a tumble of mossy rock. As we approach the summit, yellow splashes of paint, or "blazes," and large rock cairns guide us. I hike ahead for a few minutes and when I look back, I can no longer see Maegen through the fog. The steep terrain engages me and forces my calves to work like they never have before.

Round droplets of moisture cling to my fleece. Out of the fog, I spot a plaque cut into a large rock. I run my fingers over the raised text.

Marcy, also known by the Indian name Tahawus, meaning Cloud-Splitter.

I like that. *Tahawus. Cloud-Splitter, the one who splits clouds.* I wish the clouds would split now, so that I can see what's around me, but the view is obscured and I stare out at a world of gray.

After six hours of climbing, Maegen and I lean against the summit rock to eat our lunches. The absolute stillness of the world captivates me. I don't want to leave, but I know I cannot stay. From the bottom of my pack, I dig out the disposable camera and snap a photo of the gray nothingness before we descend into the mist.

After five miles downhill, the tips of my toes scream for release. I take off my shoes and settle my feet into the dark mud. The earth pushes up between my toes, and for the last two miles I run barefoot in the rain, mud splattering my legs.

Running through the mountains feels like the most natural thing in the world.

From a young age, being athletic and playing sports have been a central part of my identity. My family cultivated three main values in me and my sisters: faith, family, and sports. Believe in God, be a good daughter, and play hard. I'm not sure which came first: the knowledge that sports were important or the fact that I was a strong and competitive kid. My above-average height, broad shoulders, boundless energy, and easy speed made me a natural athlete. By the time I was thirteen, my bedroom walls were plastered with posters of Mia Hamm and Michelle Akers, two of Team USA's best soccer players.

My dream had been to play soccer at a collegiate level, possibly even to go further. But it seemed my athletic ambitions were always limited by my body. I was diagnosed with asthma before I could walk, and then ulcerative colitis, a chronic inflammation of the lower intestines, at age ten. Driven by the desire to be normal, I often refused to acknowledge the complexity of my illnesses—or the consequences of not taking care of my body. When I reached college and my mother was no longer around to manage my treatment, I stopped taking my medications. With the newfound freedom to live however I wanted, I made poor nutritional decisions that often resulted in bingeing the sugary, processed foods I'd been denied early in life. In the end, my college soccer career was lackluster. I spent most of those years inflamed and depressed.

Now on the slopes of Mount Marcy, my legs seem to go faster with every stride, and I open into a full sprint. It's a wild and uncontrolled rush. Having to focus so intensely on my foot placements as I pick my way between rocks and roots reminds me of the joy I often felt playing soccer. For the first time in years, I feel strong and powerful, not controlled by my physical limitations. I'm free.

Over the next two months, I hike twenty of the 46 Adirondack High Peaks, mountains originally measured over 4,000 feet. Every time I explore these ranges, I want to keep going, climbing up them to run down.

The miles under my feet accumulate and I develop cheap yet effective hiking systems. From the foods I eat, mainly Clif bars and apples smeared with peanut butter, to the secondhand thrift store clothes I buy. Over the summer, I save enough money to make one major gear purchase: my first trail running shoes, a pair of La Sportiva Raptors from The Mountaineer store in Keene Valley.

As the world of hiking and trail running expands before me, I see the need to take better care of myself, so I schedule a doctor's appointment to get back on my medications. I notice my body becoming strong in new ways.

I also notice the majority of people on trail are men. I start to anticipate their stares and comments when I see them coming.

"Are you hiking by yourself?"

"A woman who likes to hike? You're my kind of woman."

"My son hikes. Maybe I could introduce you."

In the beginning, I think their concern about a young woman hiking alone is an act, a comedy routine. But it isn't. Over time, I come to understand that those who hike in the High Peaks consider themselves a class above—members of an elite club. And it's a boy's club.

When male hikers aren't trying to hit on me, they're trying to outhike me. I find it laughable when they see me approaching and increase their pace. I smile as I pass by without breaking a sweat, my long legs chewing up the terrain at three to four miles per hour.

I give zero fucks. It doesn't stop me. It fuels me.

I'm going to do a lot more than just turn some heads.

At the end of my first season of hiking in the High Peaks, I share some trail miles and friendly conversation with a stranger coming off Phelps Mountain. Before we part ways in the parking lot, she pulls a newspaper from her dashboard and says, "This seems like something you would do."

The article is long and intensely detailed, recounting the recent climbing adventure of Jan Wellford and Cory Delavalle. They have just become the first to do something once thought impossible: In seven days, fourteen hours, and fifteen minutes, they connected all 46 Adirondack High Peaks in one continuous push, covering 196 miles and 70,000 feet elevation gain without any resupply or outside support. This is known as an Unsupported Fastest Known Time (FKT). There are also Self-Supported FKTs, where athletes are allowed to cache items along the route or resupply in towns along the way, and Supported FKTs, where athletes can have unlimited help from outside sources including a full crew and pacers.

Unsupported FKT immediately becomes my new sport—what I'm training for and the kind of athlete I want to be. I envision myself moving rhythmically through the mountains with long strides and everything I need to survive on my being. Those two men have no idea what they've set in motion.

I'm obsessed.

July 2012

Bags of all my favorite candy surround Daniel and me on the living room floor. It looks like Halloween exploded here in our Lake Placid apartment. We shovel handfuls of M&Ms, Reese's peanut butter cups, and gummy bears into ziplock bags. I flatten the plastic and number them one to eight in thick permanent marker, before meticulously packing them into the stiff confines of a bear canister.

Every now and again, a chocolate candy slips into my mouth, and I smile at my husband of one year. "Just trying to make our packs lighter."

"Let me help." Daniel reaches into the bag of gummy bears.

The afternoon slips by, both of us snacking and laughing as we review our gear list for the hundredth time. Tomorrow we will catch a ride to the Seward Trailhead. From there, we plan to re-create the unsupported 46 High Peaks thru-hike—and lower Jan and Cory's FKT from 2009.

Next to my composition notebook, which holds our detailed itinerary and my collection of sketches of Whiteface Mountain, lies the newspaper article about Cory and Jan that I was handed three years ago. I've been ceremoniously transporting the article like the Olympic torch from apartment to apartment, hoping I might be the next person to complete the route—and the first woman.

Almost everyone I had told about the thru-hike brushed me off with a "that's crazy" and changed the subject. Until I met Daniel at a friend's barbecue in 2010; the topic came up and he earnestly wanted to hear every detail. What was the route? What gear would I take? Maybe we could go for a hike sometime and scout a section?

To which I responded, "Sure, that sounds great."

On and off trail, Daniel and I quickly discovered we had a compatible energy. So it made sense when our friendship shifted to romantic love. Inspired by how my mind and body was transformed by hiking in the High Peaks, I found work as a field instructor for a wilderness therapy program. Every other week, I led week-long backpacking trips for teenagers who struggled with addiction, eating disorders, and mental well-being.

"Maybe I could do that too," Daniel said during our first winter together.

"Ah," I paused, soaking in the idea. Daniel had a gentleness to him I couldn't quite explain. I worried the students would sense his softness and push up against his boundaries. "Well, you can apply and see what happens."

Six months later he got the job.

What happened next was a pleasant discovery: Daniel turned out to be a natural when it came to working with these struggling teenagers. His approach was quiet, calm, and compassionate. I didn't realize early in our relationship how much trauma he carried within, but the kids could sense that he really understood them.

Our lives revolved around the mountains—living and working in them.

The following year we got engaged in a lean-to at the base of Mount Redfield. We married on a dock over Seventh Lake near the tiny town of Old Forge with amber water lapping against the sandy shoreline. We wrote our own vows, which spoke directly to our love and gratitude for each other and the place that brought us together. We promised to continue exploring, as Mary Oliver put it, "this one wild and precious life," side by side.

I glance up at our wedding photo framed on the wall, then back at the man sitting next to me with gummy bears in his teeth. I can't believe I'm getting to live out all my dreams. Taking on my biggest challenge yet, in my favorite place, with this loveable goofball by my side.

Daniel and I tighten the straps on our sixty-liter packs and set them by the door, before I curl into his long, lean frame for a few restless hours of sleep.

In the pitch-black darkness of 2 a.m., we are dropped in the parking lot with our packs. We move swiftly through the sleeping forest and greet the dawn on our first summit. By midday the temperatures are breaking into the low eighties. Sweat pours down our bodies in the late July humidity. I struggle under my fifty-pound pack and silently wish we had splurged on some ultralight gear, instead of carrying our regular wilderness therapy kits. But we had both balked at the idea of spending hundreds of dollars for lighter versions of gear we already had, especially considering what we owed in student loans each month.

Despite the weight, we're able to cover over forty miles and summit seven High Peaks, traversing the difficult terrain of the Seward and Santanoni Ranges on our first day. Around 1 a.m., we collapse in our tent, lying side by side on our ground pads without blankets or sleeping bags. We're right on schedule.

"That was ridiculous." I rest my head on Daniel's broad chest.

"So ridiculous." He chuckles.

The night air barely dips into the seventies. A hazy orange moon drifts over the mountaintops, to be replaced the next morning by an even hazier sun. While we pack up camp, I notice a throb behind my eyes and feel a dull headache coming on.

Slightly nauseous, I skip breakfast.

The heat continues to build as we walk along old logging roads. Without the protection of the forest canopy, the sunlight scorches my face and shoulders.

"You should drink more," Daniel reminds me as we rest on the banks of the Opalescent River.

"Okay." I take a few small sips, not telling him how hard it is for me to get any water down right now.

He extends our "Day 2" ziplock baggie in my direction. "Want some M&M's?"

The mere sight of the colorful candy brings bile to the back of my throat. "No thanks." I shake my head.

Daniel takes point from the river. I quickly fall behind. *What is happening?* It feels like my legs are disconnected from my head. They feel far away and impossibly heavy—I am tripping over easy rolling terrain.

I keep pushing forward, hoping to catch up with Daniel and figuring whatever is happening will eventually pass. I've never done anything this hard before and knew I would feel new sensations in the process.

But it doesn't pass.

"Daniel," I slur as we descend Allen Mountain, our first High Peak of the day. My feet stumble over the rocks beneath me.

"Here, sit here." Daniel guides me to a gentle stream, which runs alongside the trail. "Let's drink something." He is so calm, almost serene, as he offers me his water bottle. It's just like at work—only now *I* am the student.

"No," I protest.

He takes a small ziplock baggie of potato chips and crushes them between his fingers. "How about something salty?"

With his camp spoon, he brings the chips to my mouth. I don't want to let them in. The thought of anything entering my body at this point feels unbearable. I barely part my lips so Daniel can push the spoonful of chips inside. Slowly, I move them around with my tongue and swallow. The salt tastes surprisingly good.

"Let's get you in the water," Daniel instructs. "Your body needs to cool down."

Around us, the air is a stagnant ninety degrees, but Adirondack mountain streams stay cold year-round. My body convulses as I dunk beneath the water, gripped by the intensity of the temperature change.

"Ah!" I gasp as soon as I'm back above the surface. Water trickles down my face and into my open mouth. The fire burning within me cools and is slowly extinguished. I can feel my rational mind returning.

Our attempt to break Jan and Cory's record is over. Now it's easy to see that I've put us in a dangerous situation. Luckily Daniel knew what to do. Tears slip down my already wet cheeks. Daniel helps me back to shore, where we sit with our heads bowed together.

"It's okay." He squeezes my hand. "You're okay."

I resume soaking in the river until my body temperature stabilizes. Daniel sets up our tent and cooks dinner. He treats liter after liter of water with iodine, so by evening I am peeing again. The dark-brown urine that escapes my body warns of the danger I was in.

The next morning I lie in my sleeping bag, thinking maybe I am strong enough to continue. A moment of hope in the pre-dawn light. All might not be lost after an evening of recovery. But as soon as I stand and try to shoulder my pack, a wave of nausea comes over me and my legs buckle.

In the middle of our campsite, I cry into the dirt. I berate myself for not drinking enough, carrying a pack that was too heavy, and not waiting for an ideal weather window. So many mistakes. So many things I could have gotten right. I should know better. I'm a guide.

"We'll get this someday," Daniel says, one hand gently rubbing my back.

"I know." I nod sadly.

But do I even want to try again? Right now it's hard to imagine. Maybe I only gravitated toward the record because I needed a goal during a transitional period of life. I just want to go home, take a cold shower, split a margherita pizza with Daniel, and sleep in our bed. My world with him is more than enough. I don't need to make history.

August 2016

Four years later, I'm ready to try again. Turns out this record is something deeper than a crazy dream I had at twenty-three. Just like my connection to this wild land, it has become a visceral part of me.

In our front yard, Daniel and I test my newly purchased lightweight gear by propping up a nylon tarp with a set of trekking poles. Under the tarp I arrange my ground pad and bivy. I crawl in and look out at Daniel, knowing this time he won't be by my side. Since our wilderness therapy program unexpectedly closed in 2014, Daniel's own mental struggles have become more evident. It's become harder and harder to get him back to the mountains. Something I never imagined would be a challenge, or reality, for us.

Hands resting on his hips, he smiles at me. For a moment I feel like newlyweds again, brimming with hope and ideas. Earlier in the year, when I told Daniel I wanted to try the thru-hike again, he had been nothing but supportive. He began researching lighter gear immediately and purchased an aluminum cup and MSR PocketRocket camping stove, so I could boil water for dehydrated meals. But there was never a question of whether he would go with me. He wasn't in the shape he'd been in four years ago—we both knew that.

But I turned our 2012 attempt into a valuable learning experience and have been busy in the mountains ever since. Inspired by female athletes like Jennifer Pharr-Davis and Heather Anderson, who set Supported and Self-Supported FKTs on the nearby Appalachian Trail. Both beat the men to take the overall records. Both proved women are built for endurance, bucking the dominant patriarchal narrative represented on most outdoor magazine covers. Their athletic feats were the kindling keeping the fire of my dream alive.

In 2013, I set my first FKT with my younger sister, Mallory, at the Saranac Lake Ultra 6er Challenge. Over the course of six mountains and thirty miles, I felt a whole new level of empowerment. There are not many women in this sport, but I know if there were more, we'd be proving again and again what we're capable of. My confidence grows as I train my body to take on bigger miles, more challenging terrain, and longer days. I have prioritized taking better care of my asthma and ulcerative colitis, staying on top of my medications, and visiting the doctor regularly. I need my health to cover the miles I yearn for.

A vision for my future begins to blossom.

Mountain athlete. Writer.

I dream of my first shoe sponsorship and writing for *Outside* magazine, taking up space that has so far been allotted to only a small percentage of women. I want to join their ranks and show others what is possible.

As my second attempt at the thru-hike approaches, the press loves this narrative. Not only am I trying to become the first woman to hike all 46 Adirondack High Peaks unsupported, I've decided to raise money for my alma mater, where I now work, to support scholarships and sustainability programs. Still paying off student loans, I want to help young people combat the cost of a degree while using my platform to draw awareness to the environmental issues I lecture on.

The college puts out a press release, which gets picked up by major local and national networks. On top of planning logistics, strategy, food, and gear, I'm now taking on interviews and public appearances.

One outlet reaches out to request that I bring a camera to film my hike. I hesitate—the last thing I need as I attempt the hardest thing I've done so far is the extra weight of a camera and the responsibility to document my every move.

"What if I come in for sections and film it?" Daniel suggests.

"I'm not sure if it would count as unsupported."

I run the idea by Jan, one of the original record holders who over the years has become a friend and mentor. The FKT community is still rather grassroots, and some unsupported efforts have been filmed from a distance. After much debate, I agree to bring Daniel on as a cameraman and am happy that he'll be joining me for sections.

A reporter from PBS meets us at Coreys Road to film me signing in to the trail register. As I set off on the trail, Daniel falls in behind me, capturing footage of my second attempt before getting picked up at another trailhead. He pops in and out of the woods and I get to see him a little bit each day. On the second day, my body feels strong as I pass the place where he laid me in the stream in 2012, when I was overheating. I could not feel further from that novice.

"The fundraiser is over $10,000," Daniel tells me on the fifth day, before I head for Mount Marcy and the Great Range.

"That's awesome," I say, but my mind is distracted by the growing heat and humidity that crept in yesterday. Uneasiness grows every time I think back to how my first attempt ended.

Daniel and I part ways, and the temperature ticks upward. Eighties push into the nineties, and on the exposed terrain of the Great Range, which is composed of some of the highest mountains in New York, I can't think straight. Sun beats down on my shoulders. I try to take a deep breath, but the air is too hot. I hyperventilate. Shaking, I sit down beneath a fir tree in the col between Mount Haystack and Basin Mountain. But even in the shade, I'm unable to cool down. Waves of nausea wash over me.

One hundred miles and twenty-three High Peaks in, I don't want to stop, but I don't know what to do. I can't move fast in this heat, and if I can't keep moving fast, I won't be able to break Jan and Cory's record. The anxiety builds. My abdomen grumbles and the diarrhea begins. My ulcerative colitis is flaring up—I'm losing fluid faster than I can replace it and struggling to find enough places to dig catholes.

Back from yet another trip into the woods to relieve my bowels, I sit on a large rock and think about the women in my life: my mother, my sisters, my aunts, my grandmothers. I want this for them. For me. But I also know they'd want me to be safe and to take care of myself. I cry, my tears cool against my overheated cheeks. I know it's not wise to continue. My condition is rapidly declining, and I'm not able to do any of the things that would make it better. I don't want to let go. Not again. But I can't stay here. I smack my trekking poles against the rock I'm sitting on, mutter a few obscenities, and begin my descent.

From Johns Brook Lodge, a building for backcountry aid only accessible by hiking, I call Daniel.

"Oh, B, I'm so sorry."

"It's okay," I bite my lip to keep it from quivering. "Can you pick me up in Keene Valley?"

"Of course. I'll be there in thirty minutes."

"No rush," I say bitterly. "I still have four miles to hike out." Tears prick my eyes. "Thanks for all your support. You were amazing."

In the valley, the heat is stagnant, and I pull over to dig a few more catholes. Daniel greets me in the parking lot and wraps me in a hug. My head falls against his chest. Suddenly the greasy hair and dirt-encrusted fingernails I'd grown so fond of over the days feel out of place next to his recently showered body.

That night, I dream of stepping over rocks and roots. When I wake up, I can't understand why I'm not under my tarp. Then it comes back to me. I choke back my tears.

For the sake of the fundraiser, I finish the twenty-three remaining mountains as day hikes and complete the 46 High Peaks in twelve days. The last mountain I climb is Basin. From the summit, I can see the col I sat in before walking away from the record. So close, yet so far away. I snap a photo for the news outlets who still want to cover my story and move on.

That night as the hazy sun lowers, Daniel takes me out for burgers and sweet potato fries. I try to focus on the good. Like how this experience brought Daniel back into the woods with me, and how I raised money for my students. But when the glass of merlot I had with my burger leaves my system, I'm haunted. Lost. Maybe I should try again. Maybe this was never for me. Maybe there are things in life that, no matter how hard you try, you simply do not get.

June 2020

EVERYTHING IS PACKED away. Our gear room untouched. I sit in a pair of faded sweats on my queen-size bed, watching fat raindrops roll from leaf to leaf on the bright green maple tree outside the bedroom window. My laptop rests against my thighs, and I stare blankly at the screen, trying to find something meaningful to work on. After a few pained moments, my fingers tap against the keyboard, pulling up yet another *The North Face Presents* YouTube video.

In this new era of COVID-19, I feel like I'm living in slow motion. But it isn't just the pandemic; I've felt this way for a while now.

My eyes dart around the dimly lit room, and I push a strand of blonde hair behind my ear. The video ends and I flip to my Facebook page—another distraction. There's a new message from a woman named Katie Rhodes. I don't know her. A spark of curiosity—a tiny dose of dopamine hits me as I click on it.

Hi, Bethany, I stumbled upon your name while doing some research for a hike I hope to take next year. This is a personal challenge I have dreamed about, and I feel it's time. I'd like to attempt the Adirondack 46 Thru-Hike.

My shoulders straighten. I pull the laptop closer to make sure I've read the message correctly.

I scroll through Katie's profile. She's a muscular brunette with nature-themed tattoos covering her arms; vines wrap around her biceps. She carries a heavy pack in many of the photos, most taken on trails measuring over a marathon in length. The Pemi Loop in New Hampshire. The Great Range Traverse in the Adirondacks.

She's a New York State–licensed guide and the short bio beneath her profile picture reads, "I love things that seem impossible."

Let's talk! I type back, then stare at my computer screen, waiting for her to reply. This is the most excited I've been in a while. After 2016, I knew I didn't want to make another attempt at the thru-hike alone. Even though I had made it much further than Daniel and I had in 2012, the solo experience wasn't for me. Over the years since, I'd tried to find a partner but never could. A few people—all men—had expressed interest, and I spent days in the mountains completing ultra-distance hikes with several candidates, but they just didn't cut it. After twenty miles, one man told me, "Yeah, there's no way I could do this day after day."

Secretly, I wished some other woman would lower the FKT, so I could finally let it go. Tiring of the Adirondacks, I left as often as I could to climb bigger mountains and breathe more deeply. Colorado, California, Washington, Oregon, Nepal, and Argentina. Something in my life was shifting, but I was too afraid to give it a name.

Now Katie—a woman—was reaching out to me, during a global pandemic. When I least expected it. And most needed it.

I felt a familiar flutter in my stomach—one I hadn't felt in a long time.

When Jan and Cory's unsupported FKT was finally broken in 2019, I received a slew of emails sharing news links about the accomplishment: Twelve hours had been slashed off the record. Every email had ended with the same question, "So when are you going back?" Little did they know it was hard enough for me to get out of bed and brush my teeth, let alone think of hiking nearly two hundred miles in seven days.

Earlier this month, the record was broken again by three men: Michael Jaworski and cousins Dan and Paul Fronhofer. Almost another whole day comes off, lowering the time to six days, five hours and forty minutes.

A new message from Katie pops up on my screen, *Okay! When? Now?*

Sure!

At the end of our phone call, we arrange to meet and go on a four-day expedition the first week of August to scout sections of the thru-hike and see if we're a compatible team. I set aside my laptop, pull a hair tie off my wrist, and gather my hair up into a ponytail. I open my gear closet and pull out a foam ground pad, unrolling it on the floor, even though our meetup is over a month away. Then I grab the essential pieces of gear I will need for our scouting expedition and set them on the pad: headlamp, sleeping bag, tent, water purification kit, bear canister, and first aid kit.

Just the act of arranging my gear—in the same way I've been doing since my early days as a wilderness therapy guide—proves to be grounding and therapeutic. My skin prickles as I look at the framed map of the 46 High Peaks on my bedroom wall. This is why I fell in love with these mountains. This is why I stayed. I need this expedition, and I need to finish it this time. For this is all I have to connect me to the woman I once was.

September 2020

My alarm sounds at 7 a.m. Soft autumn light dapples the green carpet of the spare bedroom where I spent the night on a twin-size mattress set directly on the floor. It's stained and lumpy but compared to where I'll be sleeping for the rest of the week—on half a foam ground pad and a forty-liter pack—it might as well be a king-size bed in a five-star hotel. I take inventory of my body: muscles strong, brain well-rested, stomach ready for coffee and breakfast. I've gotten a solid eight hours of sleep.

When I was coming up in the sport of ultra hiking, I tried to mimic the 2 a.m. starting times I saw on other athlete's speed records, but they never seemed like a head start to me. A restless night of wired energy and anxiety about the approaching alarm was almost worse than no sleep at all. The early rise upended my sensitive digestive system, leading to no bowel movement (or several) and painful stomach cramps during the first day.

My strategy shifted after my two failed thru-hike attempts. I had a subtle "Ah-ha" moment: I didn't have to start FKTs at 2 a.m. or even 6 a.m. Unlike a race, I could begin the clock whenever I wanted. There are no fellow competitors toeing the start line, only me and the clock. After some experimentation, I found that late morning best aligns with my body.

I slide into my favorite ratty gray sweatshirt; the cuffs and collar are torn, and my last name is printed in blocky text across the shoulders above my high school soccer number, 15. My grandmother religiously wore it to my varsity games, cheering from the stands, loud enough I could hear her from the pitch. I've been wearing it since her vascular dementia progressed to the point that getting into a sweatshirt became too much effort for her. Though it doesn't carry her smell anymore, it's easy to feel her diehard support when I wrap myself in it.

My bare feet pad across the wooden hallway floors and Tahawus (Tuh-HAWS), my thirteen-pound terrier mix, follows a step behind me as I make my way downstairs. Daniel and I chose him after seeing a friend's terrier bomb down a ski slope five years ago. We thought he'd be the perfect adventure buddy, making us a little family for our time in the mountains.

When Daniel suggested the name Tahawus, I thought of the first time I hiked Mount Marcy in the fog and ran my fingers over the engraved plaque on the summit rock. Tahawus is a Mohawk word that roughly translates to cloud-splitter. During the nineteenth century, many locals advocated for it to become the official name of Mount Marcy, though it never did, instead retaining the name of a governor who never stepped foot on her flanks. Rolling the name over a few times in my mind, I decided the name was perfect. "I love it. Our very own little cloud-splitter."

As he grew from puppy to adult, his fur faded from dark to auburn brown, and I fell completely in love with his floppy ears and how he'd snuggle his hips into mine at any given opportunity. I always feel a little guilty leaving him behind for big adventures.

As I prepare his breakfast, I notice a folded note on the kitchen counter with a single *B* marking the front. Daniel has already headed to work and left this behind. I try to ignore the note and go about my business, setting the bowl down for Tahawus, who greedily sinks his round face into it, and making my coffee. Finally I cave and open it, thinking I should do so before Katie, who drove in from Saratoga last night and crashed in our spare bedroom, appears in the kitchen. My shoulders slump forward as I take in his familiar all-capital handwriting.

B,

YOU GOT THIS "QUEEN B" OF THE HIGH PEAKS.

GO SHOW THEM HOW IT'S DONE. I'VE ALWAYS
BEEN SO AMAZED BY YOU AND YOUR PASSION
FOR THE MOUNTAINS. I STILL REMEMBER THE
FIRST TIME YOU TOLD ME ABOUT THE THRU-
HIKE AND WE SCOUTED A SECTION TOGETHER.
THINGS WILL GET HARD, I'M SURE, BUT YOU'LL
FIND A WAY THROUGH. YOU ALWAYS DO.

I HAVE NO DOUBT THAT YOU WERE BORN TO DO
THIS.

SHOW THEM ALL HOW THIS IS DONE.

LOVE,

DANIEL

My heart aches, then anger rushes in to protect it. I try to stay angry, to avoid painful nostalgia for happier times. When we were both wilderness therapy instructors, we'd give each other notes before going to our respective groups, where we wouldn't see each other for a week at a time. When things got difficult, or lonely, those notes were a way to feel his presence, his support, and carry him with me.

But with everything that has happened in the past three years, I don't know if I can do it this time. Hell, I don't even know if I *want* to carry him with me any longer.

I hear Katie's footsteps in the guest room and stuff the note in the pocket of my sweatpants.

Katie doesn't know Daniel and I are separated. Not many people do. It's too complicated and messy, and even if I wanted to explain, I don't know if I could. I'm protective of him, and myself. It's not that we don't love each other. Sometimes it's harder than that. And I don't want Katie to think I'm distracted. That anything will keep me from our mission. I've seen people fall apart on high-stakes expeditions because of a broken heart. It's not pretty. So I've kept this part of my life to myself as we trained and planned for today. I can tell her after.

In the shower, water pounds against my back. I savor the sensation of being naked and clean, something I won't experience for the next seven days. Rose-infused soap lathers against my skin and I breathe in the hot steam. From here on out, it will be one baby wipe per day.

I dry off and put on my underwear, sports bra, tank top, and loose-fitting trekking pants. If my ulcerative colitis flares up, these will allow room for my painfully bloated abdomen. Then I climb back into my grandma's sweatshirt and twist my wet hair up into a towel. Before tossing my sweatpants in the laundry basket, I remove Daniel's note and place it between the pages of the book I'm currently reading. This time, I will not take his words with me. I can't afford their weight.

Day One

September 10, 2020
21.6 miles
7,380 feet vertical gain

Seward Mountain Trailhead (1,740 ft.)

Our journey begins at Coreys Road, a loose gravel track that weaves back into the wilderness away from New York State Route 3. For the next two days, Katie and I will travel through the most remote sections of the High Peaks. Where cell reception is lost, and the modern world is replaced by trees and rivers. Where hikers go missing, never to be found again, and rumors of Bigfoot sightings circulate. Where lumber camps were established in the 1800s to ravage the land, far from the awareness of settlers and city folk.

In winter, this section of the road remains unplowed and only accessible by foot or ski, adding to its remote allure. My minivan loops around a wide bend, navigating between deep potholes, and the towering pine forest opens. We scan the area in hopes of seeing a bear or moose. Not Bigfoot.

Early in my backpacking career, I often led students through the Seward Range as a wilderness therapy instructor. Their rugged contours are as familiar to me as my own. Having known this place as the start of the thru-hike for almost as long as I've known about the mountains, I have always felt a deep pull, like a siren's song, to these wild forests.

Just after 10 a.m., Katie and I swing into a space in the mostly empty lot, directly across from the trail register. I cut the engine, and for one brief moment, all is still. Then in unison, Katie and I open our doors to step out of the minivan. And just like that, feet replace wheels and birdsong takes over where the radio left off.

For the next few minutes, we ready our packs. This is the last time to check our gear before the clock starts. It's not a moment to rush, though our feet are eager. I slide off my flip-flops and pull on a pair of fresh socks and my new (recently broken-in) La Sportiva trail runners.

From the back of my minivan, I grab a pair of collapsed trekking poles—black and orange with the hand straps cut off to shave a few extra ounces—and adjust them to my preferred height. Katie and I share a nod as she adjusts the straps on her pack. These poles are for both of us.

Before I set out on my second attempt of the thru-hike in 2016, Jan had convinced me I would want and need trekking poles. I had never used them before and quickly hated them. They blistered my hands and tripped me up so much that I was falling on trail more than I ever had before. A few times, in angry rages, I smacked them against trees, cursing my mentor. But as I continued training, I found a rhythm and realized how invaluable they were, taking weight off my knees on ascents and descents and helping me navigate technical terrain.

This time, I was the one sharing the good word with Katie. She had resisted at the beginning of the summer when we planned our gear list, telling me she never used them.

"How about we take one pair for the two of us?" I'd suggested, knowing I didn't need them all day every day and wanting her to understand they were available to her.

Right from the beginning, I appreciated the dynamic between Katie and me. It was easy to see myself in her. Four years ago on my last attempt of the thru-hike, I was thirty, the same age she is now. I had been ambitious, bold. I didn't know what I had signed up for in many ways, but I knew I wanted to push myself. She has the same drive. Now after years as a teacher and group leader, I am excited to pass on my knowledge, but I know not to push too hard. Some things Katie will have to learn for herself, just like I did.

Above the forest canopy, a patch of blue sky shows through the low hazy clouds. The humidity is forecasted to break sometime today and then we should have a week of near perfect weather, ranging from just below freezing at night to seventies in the day, with a possible chance of rainstorms on Sunday afternoon. I strip off my grandmother's sweatshirt and leave it in the back of the minivan.

"Got everything?" I ask, surveying the seats and floor.

"I do."

"Sweet." I click the lock button on the key fob. The minivan chirps, and I stash the keys behind the back tire.

Packs in hand, we walk to the large trailhead sign, which reads:

High Peaks Wilderness Area
Seward Mtn. Trailhead.

I've been here before. Dozens of times. To guide, camp, and climb—twice to attempt the thru-hike. With Daniel and now without. My stomach flutters as I reach out to touch the soft, worn wood of the sign. *Will the third time be the charm?*

"Let's get some pictures," I suggest. "Is your phone still on?"

"Uh-huh." Katie digs it out of her pocket.

In front of the sign, I throw my hands above my head and hope this will be the last "before" photo I ever have to take here. Katie snaps the picture and we switch positions. Stretching the blue-and-white fabric in front of her chest, Katie somberly poses with a 46Climbs bandana. She looks down at the logo and parts her lips in a half smile.

46Climbs is an organization that raises funds for suicide prevention and awareness during an annual week of climbing events around the country. It started in 2014 when the cofounders attempted to hike all 46 High Peaks in one week, to honor a friend they'd lost to suicide in high school and raise money for the American Foundation for Suicide Prevention (AFSP). Their mission ended early due to malnutrition and an encounter with a black bear, but it grew into something much larger.

After taking photos, Katie ties the bandana to the outside of her pack. Early in our planning and training, Katie had confided that she had lost her older brother to suicide. When she told me she wanted to dedicate her thru-hike to him by doing a small fundraiser for 46Climbs, I readily agreed to raise money and mental health awareness with our hike, providing a spotlight on a topic that has so often been considered taboo.

I had wondered at that moment if I should reveal more of my story with Daniel, and how much I feared for him and others during this global pandemic of isolation and limited mental health resources, but I decided against it. This moment was for Katie and her brother. A valuable lesson I had learned about communication during wilderness therapy: When someone shares a trauma with you, don't immediately add yours. Listen first. Hear them. Feel their pain and honor their grief. Additionally, Daniel hadn't died by suicide, but Katie's brother had, and I hesitated to compare those two things. When someone is gone, they are gone.

Katie turns her phone off and I open the register to sign us in. Most trailheads in the Adirondacks have register books provided by the Adirondack Park Agency, which hikers use to write down the details of their itinerary. This information is helpful not only in case of search and rescue efforts but also to track the number of visitors in the mountains for resource allocation.

Using a battered pencil with barely a sliver of lead left, I scribble:

9/10/20, Bethany and Katie, one week, Seward Range and Seymour, then thru-hike all 46 High Peaks to Whiteface and Esther

Our intention has been announced. Here in this logbook, and earlier this morning on our Facebook pages. The world and this piece of paper will know if we succeed or fail. Now it will be up to the mountains to decide if we are worthy of such a feat. I close the lid and pray that we are. As an athlete, I always found it a bit egocentric to think God should get involved in my failures and victories. But in the mountains, it isn't only about winning and losing; it could also be life or death. *Okay, just watch over us and keep us safe.*

"Ready?" I turn to Katie.

"Ready." Her fingers fumble as she clips her waist belt.

"Okay." I exhale deeply. "What's the time?"

"10:15." She presses the tracking button on the side of my GPS watch, which is wrapped around her wrist. It beeps. The clock starts ticking as we step forward together.

Seward Mountain (4,361 ft.) — No.1

THE SANDY TRAIL cuts through a hardwood forest. At the end of summer, but not yet the beginning of fall, the maple and beech leaves have started to transition in color—their fading green replaced by a burnt orange. Katie hikes before me and I watch her feet dance around exposed rocks. Her athleticism is even more impressive because she only recently discovered her passion for hiking and the outdoors after taking a physical education credit in college following her emo high school days.

"Slowly, slowly," I breathe to myself as the weight of my pack settles against my back and the straps dig into my collarbone. It's a mantra I picked up from mountain guides in Nepal while spending some time on the Annapurna Circuit with Daniel in 2014. A reminder to be present as we move through these beautiful mountains, which hasn't always been easy for me to do.

Before the figurative gun goes off at the beginning of a race or FKT, pressure builds in the legs and the mind. No matter the distance, it's hard not to sprint off the starting line. But over the years, my time in the mountains has taught me what my high school track coach never could: to pace myself.

To take the overall record for the thru-hike, which currently stands at six days, five hours, and forty minutes, we'll have to average thirty miles a day at a two miles per hour pace. It may not sound incredibly fast, but when you factor in the weight of our packs plus fifteen hours of movement and ten thousand feet of vertical gain per day, it adds up. The equation also allows for a solid six hours of sleep a night and three hours for breaks and camp chores. If all goes according to plan today, Katie and I will cover approximately twenty-two miles, summit four High Peaks, and be at the Duck Hole campsite by 10 p.m. tonight.

Under the abrasive nylon shoulder straps of my pack, I adjust my tank top to create a buffer for my skin. Early on day one, the weight feels sustainable and tidily compact. I'm proud to have whittled it below thirty pounds, even with seven days of food. A huge improvement from my attempts in 2012 and 2016.

A lot of trail athletes avoid unsupported efforts because of the pack weight. It's one thing to move quickly and proficiently while wearing a running vest carrying water and a few snacks. It's a whole other beast to do it with everything you need for a week in the wilderness pounding on your back.

One mile in, Katie and I reach our first junction. I step to the right toward the Calkins Brook Trail and Katie continues straight toward Blueberry Lean-to. We pause and look at each other.

"Oh, I thought we were going up and over the range with full packs?" I try to visualize the spreadsheet where I'd recorded our itinerary in detail.

"Didn't we decide to drop our packs and do an out-and-back?" Katie asks, her eyes wide.

Shit. Traces of previous conversations circle around my racing mind. We had considered both options, and I vaguely remember neither of us having strong feelings one way or the other. My way would be slightly less mileage, taking us up Calkins Brook to the summit of Donaldson Mountain with full packs. Katie's would be a little longer, retracing our steps back over the Seward Range, but with only a daypack. In 2012, Daniel and I went up Calkins with loaded packs. In 2016, I did the out-and-back with a daypack. In the end, both options took about the same amount of time.

"No worries, let's do the out-and-back." I rejoin Katie on the main trail, making a mental note to go over the map for tomorrow once we reach our campsite tonight, so we don't end up in another situation like this.

"You sure?"

"Yeah, it will probably be better for our knees in the long run."

We both breathe a sigh of relief. Our first miscommunication handled.

We trek forward, off to a wobbly start. I wonder if Katie and I have prepared enough to undertake this journey together. Did we spend enough time talking about our options on the route? For all FKTs in the 46 Adirondack High Peaks, hikers have creative license to decide their exact route as long as every summit is reached. Most attempts have followed the same natural flow moving from west to east, because of the gentler terrain between the Seward and Santanoni Ranges, which lends itself to a faster pace when packs are loaded down. But there are still many decisions to be made along the way.

A stream crosses the trail, and I step over the clear water. I breathe deeply to calm my nerves. Katie and I will miscommunicate. That's okay. We are going to have to improvise at times. One thing I've learned about climbing mountains is that the challenges I never expected are the ones that teach me the most.

When I first applied for a job as a wilderness therapy instructor, I'd been hiking the High Peaks all summer, so I thought I was prepared for the physical rigors of the job. Plus I was a farm kid who had practically grown up lugging heavy things around outside.

As part of the job interview, applicants were required to spend four nights in the backcountry learning the therapeutic and camping skills we'd be using with our students. I quickly discovered a loaded backpacking pack was much different than the Adidas soccer pack I'd been running up and down the mountains with.

First off, I could barely pack the damn thing. In the outpost building, where we met before heading into the field for our first training session, a mound of sleeping gear, clothes, ropes, bags of oatmeal and rice and lentils, and pots and pans lay in a circle around me. No matter how hard I tried, I couldn't get everything inside the 65-liter pack. Even when I stuffed down the contents with the sole of my boot, like my father had taught me to do with trash cans, I still couldn't fit it all in. I strapped everything that didn't fit to the outside of my horrifically lopsided pack. It swung wildly as I walked, pulling the weight awkwardly against my neck and shoulders.

Later that day, we approached the Dix Range by way of a brutally steep incline and I fantasized about flinging the pack into a ravine. I wanted to stomp and rage and quit right there. But I was the only woman in my training group, and none of the men seemed to be suffering like I was. So I bit down on my lower lip and focused on putting one foot in front of the other. I wasn't going to quit in front of them. I couldn't.

On the first night, we camped on the Boquet River under 8-by-10-foot blue tarps. I struggled to tie the trucker's hitch properly and my ridgeline sagged horribly.

Upon inspecting my shelter, the instructor asked, "Are you sure you don't want help fixing that?"

"Nope," I said. "I like it like this." I crawled inside my sleeping bag, proud and exhausted. Had it rained that night, I would have been drenched. But I'd made it there, with my monstrous pack—I felt ready to face the world. Over the next four days, my calf muscles sharpened and shoulders strengthened. My knots became more proficient and my pack more tidy. During down times, I sat in silence and found peace in not moving or doing anything. My mind and body were working in ways I'd never before experienced. The growth was profound, like when the grass sprouts after the first spring rain.

On the right side of the trail, a cairn marks the start of the Seward herd path. Katie and I step off the main trail and stash our packs behind the heart-shaped leaves of a cluster of knee-high witch-hobble bushes.

"Ah, that feels good." I arch my back.

Katie pulls out our lightweight collapsible daypack and holds it open. We place two water bottles, a bag of snacks each, our cell phones, and hard shell rain jackets inside. She shoulders the small pack and takes point.

"Let me know when you want to switch," I say.

Katie nods.

The Seward Range, which consists of three High Peaks (Seward, Donaldson, and Emmons) contains many unmarked and unmaintained trails. This section is referred to on maps as a herd path, though it is well-worn and easy to follow these days, thanks to the ever-growing number of hikers exploring the Adirondacks. But easy to follow does not mean easy to navigate. Katie methodically crosses a large mudhole, stepping from rock to log to rock. I follow suit, trying my best to keep the shin-deep mud from oozing over the sides of my trail runners. For many 46ers, people who climb all the High Peaks, conditions in the Seward Range place it notably low on the favorites list.

The hardwood maple and beech forest gives way to a mix of pines and birch. We travel along a stream and pass small waterfalls. By early afternoon we hit the technical rock slabs of

Seward Mountain, and a thin film of sweat coats me.

"I thought the humidity was going to break," I complain.

"Me too." Katie's synthetic T-shirt is already rimmed with dark circles under the armpits. "Don't worry, it will."

Knowing Katie is right, I try not to waste my energy fretting. The humidity will break, but when? Today? *Tomorrow?* By then we will have summited eight mountains and covered fifty miles and be right back where I got severe heat exhaustion in 2012. Even though I've learned from my mistakes, humid days still make me anxious. Maybe we should have pushed our start back by a day. My trekking poles tick against the ground as I inventory the potential downfalls that could squash our plan. Weather, injury, bears breaking into our food canisters, asthma, ulcerative colitis, gear malfunction. Really the list is endless, but the swampy climb up Seward Mountain reminds me that both my previous attempts were ended by heat and humidity.

In wilderness therapy, it was my job to remind students to "stay in the here and now." We spoke often about how letting regrets from the past and fears for the future run our minds robs us of the present. I need to practice staying in the here and now. At this moment, with Katie, I am dripping sweat and climbing toward the first of 46 High Peaks with nothing on my back. I am making another attempt at my dream. So far everything is going okay. I allow myself a small smile. I take a deep, steadying breath and keep moving.

"I'm going to de-layer and drink some water." I know if I don't suggest a break, we might never take one. In one smooth motion, I untuck my tank top and peel it off. Air rushes to my damp skin, where it hasn't been allowed, and I feel instant relief.

Katie stops and shrugs off the daypack. With a far-off stare she sits quietly on the side of the trail and wipes sweat from her forehead, just as she had on our first practice hike together.

"I'm afraid my pace is going to slow you down," she had admitted that day, with an uneasiness about her. We were making our way up the steep slopes of Whiteface Mountain, scouting the last leg of the thru-hike.

I squatted beside her and thought for a moment about the right thing to say. Katie was not a dejected teenager discovering the pain of hiking for the first time. She was experienced, strong, and capable. I didn't want to lose her. "I know this is a lot, but trust me, our paces will even out over a hundred miles. I'm moving too fast today. I'm so excited to be out here, after being cooped up all year with the pandemic. We won't go this fast on the thru-hike."

"But you could do it faster without me." She studied her shoes.

"No, I really couldn't." I took a stick from the ground and broke it between my fingers. "And I have no interest in trying again solo. Katie, I know we just met, but you can do this. I can tell. And your pace is exactly what we need for the thru-hike."

Katie nodded seriously. "Okay."

That's when we came up with our four agreements.

1. Katie leads on the ascents and sets the pace.
2. Ascents are no place to make up time. Go slow.
3. Don't talk on the ascents. Focus on breathing.
4. Keep most breaks to five minutes and maximize time—hydrate, eat, pee, and adjust layers.

I study her face now, looking for any sign she is falling into the same thought pattern. "How are you doing?"

"Ah," she murmurs between deep breaths. "Honestly, this mountain is kicking my ass."

The ascent of Seward Mountain is a steep one, with 2,300 feet of elevation gain over two and a half miles.

"Yeah, mine too. Let's slow down. I hate this humidity." I press my tank top to my forehead and wipe away the salty film. "Let me carry the pack for the next stretch."

Without protest, she passes it to me, and I tie my tank top in a square knot to the bottom of the shoulder strap.

"I'm so glad we don't have full packs on right now," I say around a mouthful of nuts and raisins.

"Oh my gosh, me too. I'd be an absolute puddle."

After the short break, we approach the steepest section of the mountain and Katie cuts our pace in half. Slabs of wet rock stretch upward, a row of shrubby trees on each side. Fog hangs low in the heavy air as the terrain flattens, signifying that we are approaching our first summit. The temperature at this elevation is mercifully a few degrees cooler.

A sign is nailed on a stunted tree. The yellow paint reads: *Seward Mountain*.

"Woo-hoo!" I cheer. "One of forty-six!" We have been on trail for three hours and have covered seven and a half miles, slightly ahead of our goal pace.

"Forty-five to go…" Katie adds. Her voice deflates, like the gravity of what we've signed up for is only now starting to hit her.

"One mountain at a time." I remind her, feeling my own anxiety around the humidity lessen.

I glance to the northeast, where I can spot the tiny triangular peak of Whiteface, the second-to-last peak on the thru-hike, the mountain I have sketched time and time again. My very own symbol of the quest. It stands far from the rest of the High Peaks, powerful and prominent, easily recognizable from a distance with open rockslides on its western face. I remember standing here on my first attempt and trying to understand how I could ever get there in one week. It seemed impossibly far away. And even though I know it's the same exact distance as it was eight years ago, somehow it feels closer this time around.

I pull out my cell phone and turn it on. "Okay, smile."

"Seward," we say in unison.

Mount Donaldson (4,140 ft.) — No. 2
Mount Emmons (4,040 ft.) — No. 3

It's just after 1 p.m. as Katie and I make our way toward Donaldson Mountain, which is approximately one mile from the summit of Seward. From this point on, we'll have to retrace all the terrain that we cover.

I navigate the slippery descent through a chute of dark jumbled rocks, choosing the driest footholds I can find and trying not to think about the inevitable climb back up. Tiny mosses grow in the crooks of rocks where trickling water has deposited enough soil to sustain bright green life. Moving with gravity allows us to cover ground rapidly, but the descent doesn't last long. Soon the terrain levels off long enough to shake out our legs before the next uphill. I try my best to maneuver around a large pine tree obstructing the herd path, but a branch tangles in my high bun and jabs at the still-healing cut on the top of my head.

It happened a week ago when Katie and I were testing our systems on a twenty-six-mile traverse between Giant Mountain and the Dix Range. On pace to take the overall FKT for the route, we were nearing the end when I briefly glanced down at my MP3 player. My head connected with something very solid, and my upper jaw violently smashed onto my lower jaw. I stumbled forward in sudden darkness and braced my forearms against my knees. Seconds crawled by as I blinked my eyes, hoping my vision would recover. Eventually small dots of white light twinkled around me, and a blurry Katie was standing beside me with wide eyes.

"Are you okay?" she asked.

"Yeah, I think so," I said, afraid that teeth were going to tumble out of my mouth.

"Are you sure? You hit your head really hard on that fallen log." She pointed behind me, and I caught my first glimpse of the culprit that stole my perfect day.

"I'm okay," I insisted just as I felt a warm tickle on my left temple. I reached up to touch it. Blood.

"Shit." I leaned my head forward and drops of crimson splashed onto the leaves of young beech trees. From my pocket, I pulled a spare COVID mask and cupped it to my bleeding forehead. "I'm good, let's keep going."

"Are you sure?"

"Yeah, the clock's still ticking." I stepped forward and the wound pulsated. I had to keep moving; we were still two miles out, and I wanted to ensure we took the overall record from the men.

Katie eyed me with concern, her Wilderness First Responder–brain going into overdrive. I opened my stride and began to jog, showing her that I was okay and it would take more than a downed tree to stop me.

Eventually, the bleeding stopped, and I was left with a goose egg and an inch-long gash on the side of my forehead. And a humble reminder to not look down when changing my music. But, we took the overall FKT and both felt a deep confidence in ourselves as a team. We saw how we reacted in a moment of crisis. We knew we'd be each other's lifelines out there. We were ready.

"Ow." I break off the annoying twig and keep moving, the sap sticking to my hair. Gingerly, I feel for my scab, making sure it's still intact. The rough edges itch when I touch them. Afterward, I check my fingertips for blood and I'm pleased to see none.

Twenty-five minutes later, we're standing on the summit rock of our second High Peak, Donaldson.

"Do you see a sign?" Katie asks, spinning in a circle.

I take out my phone for a summit photo and look around. To the west, the fog has lifted to reveal an open view of Seymour Mountain across Ouluska Pass. That will be our final peak of the day.

"Oh no." I point to a soggy piece of cardboard with "Donaldson" scribbled across it in marker.

"Poor sign." Katie frowns, holding the sad sign up for a photo.

Behind me, two well-seasoned hikers emerge from the dense forest.

"Good morning," says an older woman from under a ballcap. "Or I suppose it's afternoon by now?"

"It all blends together out here," I agree. We take a few steps away from the summit, allowing them space as Katie and I mask up.

"Are you doing Emmons too?" I ask, knowing many hikers pair the two mountains together.

"Yes." The second woman nods, her gray curls bouncing. "But not as fast as you two. We're just a couple of old ladies." She sets a large pack down.

"Well, we're traveling a lot lighter," I offer, not wanting them to consider either their age or their pace a diminishment of their accomplishment. They're out here hiking the same mountain we are. Another example of strong women challenging the narrative, who I'm sure faced a lot more criticism when they first pursued the sport.

The truth was that I had struggled with the fear of aging at times. As soon as I turned thirty, I felt like the hourglass had flipped, and I needed to get the thru-hike done sooner rather than later. As a young athlete, I heard—and believed—that females peak in their teens and twenties. I feared that, with the stroke of a clock, my knees would suddenly hurt all the time, and I wouldn't be able to recover from injuries. But those were all lies.

If anything, at thirty-four, I feel stronger. I'm training smarter, drawing on all the lessons learned through mistakes in my twenties. I'm taking better care of my asthma and ulcerative colitis and my nutrition is the best it's ever been. I've probably got decades more climbing in my future. If these ladies are any indication.

"Enjoy the rest of your hike." Katie waves as we leave the summit and make our way back to the main herd path.

In the process of navigating a series of dodgy mudholes, we steady ourselves against tree trunks, occasionally walking away with a scratched arm.

On a drier and easier-to-navigate section, Katie asks, "Can I get a granola bar from the pack?"

"Sure." I swing the daypack to the front of my torso, unzip it, and pull out Katie's snack bag without losing any momentum in my forward stride. I extend the bar behind me, like a runner would pass a baton in a relay race. As we approach our ten-mile mark, I'm not particularly hungry, but I open my snack bag too, knowing I need to stay ahead of the curve. I break off half my peanut butter and jelly wrap and take small bites as we move toward Mount Emmons, which lies only a mile to the south.

At 2:15 p.m., one hour after our first summit, we arrive at our third peak. Through a narrow opening in the dense pine tree cover on the summit of Mount Emmons, I look back toward Seward Mountain. "Five-minute break?" I suggest.

"Sounds good." Katie grabs her phone to check in with her

husband, Kenny.

I sit to stretch my calves while sending a text to my group chat, which I'd created earlier that morning at my house, so I could update my closest friends and family members as efficiently as possible. It was also part of our safety plan. At least once a day, we'd provide those following us with our location, should something happen and we need rescue. *Seward, Donaldson and Emmons are complete. On to Seymour.*

"Wow," Katie says. "The fundraiser is almost to $1,000."

"Whoa, that's great!"

"Looks like Kenny shared it on Facebook and 46Climbs and some other groups are sharing it." Katie keeps studying her phone. "He's trying to increase the goal amount and not sure how to do it."

Tying an FKT to a fundraiser can be inspiring. But it can also add a lot of mental pressure and become draining. By the time I started my second thru-hike attempt in 2016, I was so tired from all the publicity work that getting on trail and out of cell service was a welcome blessing. Right now, Katie and I need to conserve every bit of our energy, even our brainpower. I can see her being sucked in as the seconds tick by.

"Hey, Katie." I wait until she makes eye contact before continuing. "Kenny's got this. He's our hype man. All we have to do is hike and send him an update once a day."

"Yeah." Katie nods and clicks off her phone.

"I bet it will get sorted out by the time we reach Seymour." I pass her water bottle over. We've got miles to go, back over the summits we've already climbed to reach our packs. Then one more mountain before we're able to rest for the night. "Keep drinking, keep eating, keep hiking."

"Yes, you're right." Katie exhales.

I push myself up from the summit rock and brush pine needles off the back of my trekking pants. "And enjoy this! We're out here doing it!"

"I know, right?" Katie shakes her head in awe. "This is actually happening."

Seymour Mountain (4,120 ft.) — No. 4

BACK AT THE cairn, Katie and I pull our packs from the bushes. Katie grabs a handful of granola from her bear canister, and I offer to fill up our empty water bottles in a nearby stream.

My muddy trail runners straddle the clear water and within seconds, our hydration is resupplied and dropped with iodine tablets. While we were in the planning phase of the thru-hike, we went back and forth on what we would use to treat our water against giardia and other water-borne illnesses. Iodine tablets, Aquamira drops, ultraviolet pens, or filters? In the end iodine won, because it was the lightest and fastest option.

Katie looks up from her open bear canister. "Need any food?"

"No, I'm good for now." I lay the cool water bottle against the back of my neck.

I put my tank top back on and we strap into our packs. The weight feels cumbersome, though we will be dropping them again in half a mile at the Seymour herd path. Side by side, Katie and I walk down the remnants of an old truck trail that runs all the way to Cold River, one of the most remote wilderness areas in the Adirondacks. After the out-and-back to the summit of Seymour, we'll follow this trail to Duck Hole to camp for the night. Compared to the muddy herd paths of the Seward Range, this gravel track is luxurious.

Within ten minutes, we reach the next cairn marking the Seymour herd path and find another patch of bushes to hide our packs. Adding one water bottle for both of us to the daypack, we set off.

Mindlessly I follow Katie's Altra shoes over streams and through mudholes. Brilliant red maple leaves stand out atop the dark earth where they have fallen. I think of my mother, who loves the colorful leaves of autumn. Though there is time to observe, admire, and experience the little beauties of the mountains on this adventure, there is not enough time (or phone battery) to take photos along the way. I will have to keep these memories for myself.

Luckily the terrain isn't as muddy as the Seward Range, and we make good time for the first mile of ascent. Then with half a mile to go, we encounter steep rock slabs, which rip open the dense forest. Water trickles down the cracks of the slabs and red algae grows along the moisture. Each year, trees have fallen, their shallow roots no match for windstorms in the mountains, and the slabs have expanded in width.

"Slowly, slowly." I meditate at the base of the first one and exhale deeply.

Just after 5 p.m., the heat of the day is finally starting to wear off. My thighs and calves are fatigued from the steep incline and I pause, leaning forward on my trekking poles to stretch. In the northern sky, I find the discernible triangular peak of Whiteface again. I close my eyes and envision us on the summit, five days from now. *See it. Feel it. Do it.*

On the summit of Seymour Mountain, Katie grabs the 46Climbs bandana from her pocket and holds it across her chest. A soft breeze refreshes our tired bodies, and the sun lowers in the west.

"Number four." I snap the summit photo.

"And only forty-two to go." Katie adds. Her voice is more confident than this morning at the top of Seward, which already feels like a lifetime ago.

Just after 6 p.m. Katie hands me my headlamp from the daypack and hangs hers around her neck. "Let's get down the slabs before it gets too dark."

We are both aware most injuries happen on descents, when gravity's working with you and muscle fatigue against you. Encroaching nightfall doesn't help. The fall equinox is around the corner, meaning we have about thirteen hours of light at our disposal each day. Even though it's less than we would have in midsummer, I don't want another run-in with the heat and humidity in July and August. Luckily on the slabs, there is still enough light to see without using our headlamps, and we carefully pick our way down to our packs without a single stumble or ankle roll.

At our packs, we mechanically repeat our systems: I take our water bottles to the stream for a refill and Katie breaks out the snacks. I mix Tailwind carbohydrate powder into my water without even looking at the package. Katie recently introduced me to the wonder of liquid calories. Katie hands me a granola bar and I shove it into my mouth. I want to get as much in as possible before bed, so my body can recover. Away from the stream, I crouch in the bushes and pee. I glance downward to observe the color, a healthy yellow for the number of miles we are doing. From a nearby witch-hobble bush, I grab a leaf and wipe before shouldering my pack. When the straps settle against my collarbone, I feel like a horse who has been running free for hours and now has a rider and saddle on her back.

On the truck trail, we hike side by side, our headlamps bobbing with each step. We pass through an old lumber camp where a pair of empty lean-tos now reside. Next to them is a small meadow and a hitching post for horses. There are few trails in the High Peaks where horses can still be ridden. A metal horseshoe hangs on the side of the second lean-to—an omen of good luck.

A mile from Duck Hole, Katie and I pass over Cold River on a suspension bridge. The treated lumber smells faintly of oil, as we cross over the churning darkness below. Across the bridge, the truck trail narrows into a single sandy track. The quiet wildness of this place allows my mind to wander, turning beds of light green moss, illuminated by my headlamp, into a fantastical land. This place is magic, but not in the Bigfoot and ghosts of lost hikers way that scares people on their first night in the woods. More like forest fairies in their mossy houses and little gnomes running across the trail right when you're not looking.

Around 10 p.m. we arrive at Duck Hole and find the designated camping area empty. In one of the two lean-tos, Katie fires up the stove to boil water for our dehydrated meals. I walk around barefoot, allowing my feet to decompress from the long day. In an impromptu aromatherapy session, short balsam needles stick to the bottom of my feet, and the cool earth soothes the acute inflammation in my toes.

That first summer I hiked in the High Peaks, I completed three of them barefoot. I didn't even think of bringing a pair of shoes should I need them. My feet had such thick calluses that they never tore or blistered. But that all changed when I had to wear boots with full ankle coverage for wilderness therapy.

"Really, we can't go barefoot? Even in camp?" I asked the senior instructor when I was directed to put on my shoes.

"No, it's a huge liability," he said matter-of-factly.

"But this is a *wilderness* therapy program. Being barefoot should be a part of that."

"Yeah, our insurance company doesn't see it that way."

Begrudgingly I complied, and my feet adapted to boots, losing most of their calluses. By having to endure the confines of stiff leather, they became tough in a different way, like my body under the weight of a fifty-pound pack. And I entered a new phase of my career, going from my hippy camp counselor roots to an outdoor professional who followed insurance company rules, whether I agreed with them or not.

I dig my bare feet into the hard-packed ground surrounding the lean-to, thankful I still have a strong minimalist side that wants little to do with material things and comforts. When I met Daniel, I appreciated that we had this in common. While the water boils, Katie and I lay out our ground pads and sleeping bags in the lean-to.

"What do you want tonight?" Katie asks, grabbing a few of her homemade dehydrated meals. Before the thru-hike, she loaded me up with samples of what she could make for our dinner options.

"Um, how about the Thanksgiving dinner?" I say, suggesting my favorite.

Katie unzips a baggie and pours the boiling water directly into it. Carefully, she pinches the top of the bag closed. While the food rehydrates, we stretch on our ground pads. I massage my thumbs into the tight fascia of my calves. I lie back and do a body scan. I take a deep breath in and push it out. Lungs are clear. Good. Digestive system feels strong. No cramps. No pain. Good. No blisters on feet. Good.

"How's your body feeling?" I ask Katie.

"No complaints." Katie scoops out a portion of the Thanksgiving dinner for herself and hands me the rest. "It honestly feels like a regular hiking day."

After letting it cool a few seconds on my spoon, I take a bite. A savory blend of mashed potatoes, gravy, peas, and carrots, either sourced from local stores or Katie's garden. "Oh, this is so good."

Katie agrees with her eyes while her mouth is full of food. The satisfaction of completing our first day only adds to the taste.

After dinner, we load our bear canisters and stow them a good distance from camp, in case a black bear tries to break into them. Behind the lean-to, I peel off my hiking clothes, wipe my face, pits, and groin with a single baby wipe, and change into my polypro leggings and clean fleece. With the baby wipe in hand, I trek over to my bear canister and pull out a small ziplock bag. I fold the wipe into a cube and deposit it in the bag. Everything we carry in, we have to carry out.

From the crossbeam of the lean-to, I hang my hiking outfit to air-dry overnight. Then I grab my remaining clothes and ball them into a stuff sack, to act as a pillow. I slither into my thin forty-degree sleeping bag and lie on my back. The wooden floor is hard against my aching body, and I struggle to find any comfort on top of my empty pack and ground pad. I roll to the side, but my hip bone digs into the floor.

"Good job today," I say to Katie and click off my headlamp, settling my face against my makeshift pillow.

"You too, good night."

In the darkness of the lean-to, I close my eyes, exhaling slowly and hoping for sleep to come. But while Katie peacefully snores, I quietly toss and turn. An hour passes and I'm still awake. *Maybe it's the lean-to, maybe it's too hard. No, I've slept in lean-tos hundreds of times and never had this issue. Maybe it's trying to sleep on a pack and half a ground pad, dang ultralight gear.* As softly as I can, I tiptoe out of the wooden structure with my sleeping bag and find a flattish place on the earth to lie down. I look up into the canopy of pine trees. Stars shine between gaps in the needles. My legs are jittery; I want to move. It doesn't feel like I've hiked twenty miles today. It doesn't feel like I've hiked at all.

What's going on? Do I just have adrenaline? Is it because my body has been in rest mode the last week, tapering, and now I'm in go mode? My body stirs for another hour, and I wiggle out of my sleeping bag to pee yet again. I squat and watch the clear fluid flow into tiny rivers over the compact earth, adjusting my feet so they don't get splashed. I marvel at the amount of pee; it's a lot, like I had caffeine or something. But I haven't had any since my morning coffee. *Oh wait, the Tailwind.* I remember Katie telling me there are caffeinated flavors. I didn't read the packet when I added it to my water bottle.

"Shit," I mutter and shift my bare feet again.

Besides a few strategic sips of coffee on mornings when I need help to get things moving, I don't usually consume caffeine, so I'm wired. I glance at my watch; it's 1 a.m. I doubt I'll get any sleep tonight.

An hour later, at 2 a.m., after peeing for the third time, I consider waking Katie up two hours early to hit the trail but decide against it. She needs her sleep. And even if I can't sleep, at least I'm resting my body.

In addition to our hiking agreements, Katie and I came up with four rules surrounding self-care:

1. Take care of your feet.
2. Eat 3,000 calories a day (even if you aren't hungry).
3. Drink five to six liters of water a day.
4. Sleep six hours (or at least be off your feet and out of your socks).

An owl hoots from far away. A jumping mouse springs across the forest floor, rattling the fallen leaves and sounding far bigger than it actually is. The stars rotate above me. *Find a constellation,* I tell myself.

The first night in the woods was always the hardest for my wilderness therapy students. In the pitch-black darkness of a six-million-acre wilderness, their minds often spiraled. *It's too dark. It's too quiet. I can't be here. This is too hard.*

Ten years ago, under these same stars, one of my students was struggling to sleep. In the wee hours, she told me, "I was raped at a camp in the woods." Her perpetrator had been a family friend, and she'd never told her parents. That night, another instructor and I sat with her, quietly adding sticks to the fire while the other students slept. The best we could do was to make sure she knew she wasn't alone in the darkness.

After a long silence, she peered up and asked, "How many constellations do you know?"

"Not many," I admitted. "But let's see if we can find Orion's Belt."

Together, we searched through the oval-shaped beech and star-shaped maple leaves for three perfectly aligned stars. But our view was too limited, so we settled on making our own constellations. A dragon, a bird, and an old woman kept us company throughout the dark night.

Find a constellation, make a constellation. You're off your feet and your body is resting.

In the indigo shade of 3 a.m., I find a flower in the few stars visible to me and my mind begins to relax. My body follows suit.

Be here. Be now.

Morning will come.

Day Two

September 11, 2020
31.1 miles
8,630 feet vertical gain

Duck Hole Campsite (2,162 ft.)

"How'd you sleep?" Katie asks while we pack up camp by headlamp, preparing for the thirty-mile day ahead of us.

"Uh . . ." I pause, wondering if I should spin the truth, but then decide against it. "I didn't."

"At all?"

"No." I shrug, trying to play off the last six hours as lightheartedly as I can. "I think my Tailwind was caffeinated."

"Oh no." Katie gasps.

"It's okay," I assure her. "I'll look at the labels more closely today and make sure I cut off the caffeine by 3 p.m."

"Sorry," Katie says. "I should have reminded you about that. I know it's your first time using Tailwind."

"Really, no worries. I feel fine." In all honesty, at this moment, I do. I'm not tired and having been restless all night, I'm relieved to be up and moving. I stuff my sleeping bag down in my pack and volunteer to retrieve the bear canisters.

The beam of my headlamp bounces unevenly over the forest floor as I scan for our canisters. Finally the light catches on reflective tape, like the glimmer of an animal's eye. With the quarter I keep in the side pocket of my pants, I unscrew the top and rummage through my food for a small ziplock bag of sticky dried prunes. I pull two of them apart and push them into my mouth, not savoring them for their taste but appreciating what they will do. Whenever I hike or go on expeditions, I pack things to help me poop and things to stop me from pooping too much. Trying to be a competitive athlete with ulcerative colitis, which causes small sores—or ulcers—to form on the lining of the large colon, is like a constant game of roulette. I never know which way my stomach will go until I'm on trail. This morning it's prunes. Tomorrow might be Imodium.

When my symptoms first appeared at age ten, I would bite down on a towel so no one could hear me whimpering in the bathroom. Hot, sharp pain cut through my abdomen and the toilet water turned red. Sweat beaded on my forehead and black spots clouded my vision. I told no one. I'd been hospitalized once for four days after an asthma attack, and the thought of being trapped with doctors and IVs again scared me more than the pain I was experiencing. Also, I had heard that when girls reached a certain age, they bled. My older sister was going through that around this time. I thought perhaps I was getting my period too.

One day, my mother pushed the bathroom door open before I had time to flush. She was onto me. I was covering my symptoms as well as a ten-year-old can, but I'd been losing weight for months and spending too much time in the bathroom. My complexion was pale. My rambunctious energy was nowhere to be found.

"How long has there been blood?" she asked.

My secret was out.

"I don't know," I lied, looking away from the bloody toilet water.

"Well, we have to go to the hospital," she said matter-of-factly.

"No," I pleaded and began to cry, but my mother, who was also a nurse, stayed calm and steadfast.

"Bethany, we have to go," she said. "You can bring one of your stuffed animals."

A white seal pup with blue plastic eyes accompanied me to the emergency room. By the end of the pokes, pricks, tubes, and enemas, I was the second-youngest case of ulcerative colitis ever diagnosed in New York State. Throughout the rest of my childhood and adolescent years, my mother was my champion, my rock. She took me to all my doctor's appointments and researched GI diseases and nutrition.

Sometimes, I yelled at my mother for making me take my medication, go to my doctor's appointments, and eat non-processed, bland, boring food. I hated when she dropped me off at a friend's birthday party with a baggie of unappetizing all-natural muffins. It's never harder to appear normal than when you're surrounded by kids eating frosty pieces of cake, while you're picking off a bit of stale muffin.

When I felt sorry for myself and my limitations, she'd say, "Well, you can either get stuck in it, or it can make you stronger. God gave you this. It's a part of you and your purpose."

She tried her best to keep me well, which was hard enough. But the real anger came when all the restrictions and medication weren't working. When my ulcerative colitis flared up, the pain was nauseating, rippling through me with a burning intensity. My body would become so fatigued I couldn't even kick a soccer ball. That's when I'd stop being angry at her and start yelling at God.

It wasn't until I began hiking the High Peaks at age twenty-three that I began to tap into my own strength. Alone on the trail, I spent a lot of time talking to God and trying to understand my life and purpose. My mom had told me being sick was a part of that. It was too hard to see it as a kid who just wanted to be like everyone else. But in the mountains, I started to understand. I no longer had to do what my mom said, which only led me to realize she was right. If I took care of myself—eating the right foods and taking my medication—I could go farther and faster. What I had viewed for so many years as a weakness to be hidden from others was actually my superpower to be shared with the world.

When it came time for Katie and me to devise a food plan for the thru-hike, I knew packing enough food was only half of the equation. Packing the *right* food that wouldn't trigger a flare-up was the other.

I stuff the prunes back in the bear can between my daily bags of food, each labeled in permanent marker, "Day 1" to "Day 7," and roughly containing 3,500 calories. It's not as much as we are burning, but it's enough to get us through.

I drop the food at the lean-to and return to the privy, which is basically a square box with an oval hole cut out in the middle. I sit on the damp wood, and a small bowel movement falls into the mound of human excrement beneath me. It's not much, but it's something and eases my mind after a sleepless night.

Perhaps the biggest battle of living with a digestive disease is the fear and anxiety that comes with it. The next flare-up is a ticking time bomb, but I can never see the countdown clock. I can never know how good I will feel on a given day—even when I've done everything right. Some days are 70 percent, some are 95.

With packing finalized, Katie and I sweep the camp with our headlamps.

"Alright, looks like we have everything." I clip my waist belt and chest strap.

Katie holds up her wrist, starting our GPS track for the day. The watch beeps and we leave camp. From the shelter of the forest, we emerge into an open meadow. Knee-high grasses brush softly against our legs. Crickets chirp and I glance up at the blanket of stars and constellations above us—4 a.m. is a shade of melancholy.

By the light of our headlamps, Katie and I carefully pick our way across the broken remnants of Duck Hole Dam. With my trekking poles, I steady myself and poke at a slanted beam before transferring my weight to it. I feel like I'm walking through the skeleton of a shipwreck. When the dam was intact, a large pond covered the landscape and provided an ideal backcountry fishing location.

Years ago, Daniel and I spent the second night of our honeymoon camping by the meadow at Duck Hole, in a new L.L.Bean tent and a pair of down sleeping bags we'd gotten as wedding presents. The trip was the culmination of our goal to become 46ers together.

That night we ate dinner on the still-intact dam, gazing out over the shallow pond and daydreaming about our future together. We talked about attempting the thru-hike as partners and imagined him by my side at the finish line.

The sun lowered in the western sky as we lay on our backs, looking up at the emerging constellations.

"My favorite is Cassiopeia." Daniel pointed out a *W* shaped by five bright stars.

"Oh, that's beautiful. Maybe we can name a little girl that someday."

"And maybe for a boy, Orion."

"I like that, but let's not have kids until our thirties." I laughed.

"Agreed." I loved that he understood there was still so much to do first.

In the stars, I could see our future. Daniel and me, our adventures, our children, our life. It was as beautiful and perfect as the night sky was bright and luminous.

Two weeks later, Hurricane Irene blew through, and the dam Daniel and I had lain on was torn apart. It was never repaired.

Today a gentle river snakes through the clearing, which is beginning to refill with grasses, shrubs, and saplings. The air is damp and foggy with a tinge of humidity. It's still warmer than I'd prefer. Banks of green peat moss grow on each side of the narrow footpath. The next few miles of trail are scarcely traveled and hard to follow in sections.

"Oh no, over here. It goes this way," I say, stopping the couple of times we lose the trail to retrace our steps. Regardless of the poor trail conditions, we make good time and cover the three miles in an hour. The faintest light has found the sky. We quietly shuffle into the dawn, arriving at the base of the Santanoni Range.

Panther Mountain (4,442 ft.) — No. 5
Couchsachraga Peak (3,820 ft.) — No. 6
Santanoni Peak (4,607 ft.) — No. 7

Four miles into our day, I can't tell if it's lightly sprinkling or just drops of dew on the shore of Bradley Pond. Either way, my clothes, still damp from yesterday, are sticking to my body. I'm running on no sleep. I've failed twice at this thing I've set out to do, and I have two chronic illnesses that could go south at any point. On top of that, I'm thirty-four with puffy sleep-deprived eyes. I'm crusty, stinky, dirty, and I'm sure my hair is a mess. We're in a fucking pandemic, and it feels like everything in my life is coming to an end. I don't know what will happen when I get back home to my husband, and it feels like it might be easier to stay in the woods forever. I'm only getting older and don't have countless opportunities to keep trying this hike again and again. No one does. As much as I want to believe we're going to make it, Katie and I might fail.

This hike has been hanging over my head for a decade now, and I want to finish it so I can move on with my life. Even though I have no idea what that will look like.

"Let's stash our packs over there." I point to a round hump of earth to the side of the herd path.

Last night at the lean-to, Katie and I went over our plan for day two and we've decided to save our knees by doing the three peaks of the Santanoni Range with daypacks, like we did yesterday in the Seward Range.

"Do you mind taking the pack first?" I ask Katie. "I'm struggling a bit mentally."

"No problem." Katie offers me a smile. "Must be frustrating to not have slept at all."

"Yeah, and this fog is bumming me out." I scowl at the sky.

"I get it." Katie's compassion gives me a little boost.

I'm well aware that time on trail is a series of highs and lows. Right now I'm on a low. Katie seems to be on a high. Thank goodness—we're balancing each other out. That's why I didn't want to make another solo attempt. My mind would have gotten the best of me in the low moments. Growing up in team sports, I'm stronger when there is someone by my side.

Eight years ago, and in this very spot, Daniel was that person. The thought crashes through me. Always smiling, always positive. But that was a long time ago.

Now I'm here with Katie—a badass mountain woman. The idea of finally completing this goal with her is more than I could have ever hoped for. I watch the powerful muscles in her legs flex as she sets a conservative pace toward Times Square, a multi-directional junction from which we will complete an out-and-back jaunt to each peak. She knows I'm in a bad way this morning: tired, grouchy, frustrated. Her slow pace is an act of kindness. She doesn't realize that being out here at all is the truest act of kindness.

I unwind my headphones and tuck them into my ears, hoping to lift my spirits. Music has a way of calming my mind and connecting it to the universal picture of life. This little yellow MP3 player only contains a few hundred songs, but it has traveled to the Himalayas, Andes, Cascades, and Sierra Nevada.

I scroll to a playlist dubbed "46" and push play. As the first few chords of Pearl Jam's "Better Man" reverberate in my ears, I'm transported to someone else's story. Someone else who doesn't seem to know what to do. Not me. A character entwined in the universal saga of broken love. Of staying, because it's easier than leaving. A minute in, the beat picks up and I'm not even listening to the lyrics anymore. The guitar and drums, the melody, all of it gives me energy. As we move up the mountain, my head sways to the beat and I tap my fingers against the trekking poles. Hiking feels like dancing—my feet move to the tempo. Song after song, I escape into the music.

I haven't failed at this adventure twice before. I'm simply on an adventure. I'm not just another woman mourning her broken heart in the mountains. I'm a warrior.

The fog lifts to reveal glimpses of a blue September sky as Katie and I climb a spine of rock to summit Panther Mountain. Wolves and panthers used to roam these woods before they were hunted to extinction in the late 1800s. Another casualty of the influence of man, remembered only in name. We break through the treeline, pause, and look over our shoulders. Banks of fog roll over the mountains in the distance, creating an ocean of white in the valley. To the east, the sunrise casts a warm orange glow on the highest mountaintops, emerging from the clouds like scattered islands.

My puffy eyes lift to the sun. I exhale. There is a crispness in the air; the humidity is breaking. My sleep deprivation no longer phases me. I've done harder things. It's easy to forget gratitude, but I know this is precious. We are out here in this place I love. On the summit Katie pulls the 46Climbs bandana from the daypack and holds it in her hands. I turn on my phone and take a picture. With a few bars of cell service, I send a text message to our group chat.

Beautiful morning on Panther! Day Two has begun. Plan for the day: Santanoni Range and Allen.

At 8 a.m., I can envision each person in their daily routine. In his flannel pajamas, my father is eating a bowl of bran flakes; my mother will still be sleeping for another hour. My Uncle Bobby, who became a 46er in July (with a little of my help) is in the forest preparing his woodshed for the coming winter. My grandparents are still sleeping too, and I know they won't rise until about noon. They don't have cell phones, but I know my updates will filter into their worlds, and they will look out the kitchen window toward the blue Adirondack Mountains and know what Katie and I are doing. I have endless memories of watching the fog burn off the mountains from their garden, long before I knew what that fog felt like. Now I am here. With each minute, the blue sky expands and more mountains come into view.

The wilderness before me stretches in every direction. To the west, I locate the tree-covered summit of Seward Mountain rising above the cloud bank and think about when these forests were being clear-cut by lumber companies. Not many people know the 46 High Peaks played a crucial role in saving and preserving them. And I can't help but wonder, what would have happened if that had continued? After the Civil War, while many areas of the Adirondack Forest were being cleared to aid in the reconstruction of the country, a real estate lawyer by the name of Verplanck Colvin set out to survey the mountains. In 1870, he made the first known ascent of Seward Mountain and noted how the forest was decimated from logging. Concerned by the charred landscape, he wrote a report noting how this growing deforestation would impact much of New York State's watershed if it continued unabated. The vitality of the Hudson River, which supplied New York City with water, and the prosperous Erie Canal, which ran from Albany to Buffalo, were both highlighted in the report. After decades of lobbying by Colvin and other environmental activists, a line was drawn around the mountains to protect the watershed, and in 1892, a park was born. Today encompassing six million acres, roughly the size of the state of Vermont, the Adirondack Park is a global case study of how people can live and recreate in a protected place.

After a quick water break and snack, Katie and I descend back to Times Square. Without any signs, the jumbled intersection can be confusing to first-time hikers, but I've been here many times before. We veer to the right to take the trail to Couchsachraga Peak, whose name means "dismal wilderness."

In the world of 46ers, there are a lot of complaints about Couchsachraga. First being that it's not even 4,000 feet high. Measuring only 3,820 feet, it's the smallest of the 46, but not the only one falling short of the height requirement. Back in 1925 when Bob and George Marshall, with their guide Herb Clark, became the first hikers to complete the 46, it was believed all the peaks were over 4,000 feet. Years later, when the peaks were more accurately measured, and found wanting, the 46ers organization kept the original list intact for historical purposes.

The second complaint about Couchsachraga concerns its notoriously mucky bog with floating logs. Depending on the season, and how much rain the area has received, it can be a terrifying and disgusting place. Any misstep could land you knee-deep or face-first in muck. On top of all that, it's a mile and a half to the top, with not much to see once you get there.

Fortunately Katie and I have been riding a flow state since coming off the summit of Panther, and Couchsachraga's winding nature provides a perfect opportunity to check in.

"Want to do a feelings check?" I ask.

"Sure. What do I start with, physical?"

Feelings checks are an old tool from my wilderness therapy

days. Daniel and I used to do them on trail together and with our students. Katie and I had a lot of getting to know each other to do in a short period of time, and our ability to assess each other's states is critical to the mission, so I'd introduced them to her on our first hike.

"Yeah, let's start with physical," I say.

"I feel really good," Katie starts. "Amazing actually. No pain, no soreness. Yesterday, I was worried about how I'd feel today, but I feel so much stronger than I thought I would. How about you?"

"I feel much better. This morning I felt like my eyes were really puffy, but overall my body feels strong, and my energy is pretty high for not getting any sleep."

I lower my butt to the ground and scooch down a wet staircase of rock. My legs swing over the final lip of stone, and I jump a few feet to reconnect with the compacted trail.

"What's next?" Katie asks, turning back to look at me. "Mental. What are you thinking about?" I brush pine needles and leaves from the back of my pants.

"Oh, I've been thinking about my brother a lot. When we were kids. I really feel him out here."

Light cuts through the pine forest as I think of the picture Katie posted for the 46Climbs fundraiser. Two little kids dressed to go play in the snow, both with ear-to-ear grins.

We hop over a fallen pine tree and pick our way down to the bog. The thick brown sludge smells like a chicken coop. The summer has been relatively dry, so we are able to follow a clear path from log to log. I pass one of the trekking poles to Katie so we both have three points of contact. Our conversation stalls as we focus fully on keeping our feet above water, but occasionally, the putrid liquid seeps against my shoes.

On the other side of the bog, I resume our feelings check. "I've been thinking a lot about the weather," I say. "I was hating it this morning, but now I'm loving the bluebird sky and I'm thankful the humidity has pushed out." I don't mention how much Daniel has been on my mind; instead, I prompt the next part. "Emotionally, what do you feel?"

"Happy. Content," Katie says. "You?"

"I was worried, but now I'm feeling more peaceful and confident. I think because of my failed attempts in 2012 and 2016, I fear the weather will turn on us." I peer into the forest. The stunted trees look like little aliens with long scraggly arms and crazy hairdos. "Okay, last question. Spiritually, what are you connected to?"

"The mountains. Being here," Katie says without pause. "My brother."

"When we were on the summit of Panther, I felt connected to the fog and my family. And the heavens."

"Yeah, that's when I was really thinking about him."

The silence of reflection surrounds us. That's the thing about a feelings check; it aligns your whole being. As we make our way to the tree-covered summit of Couchsachraga, we climb between two large rocks, and a shaft of light touches Katie's shoulder. I imagine her brother walking beside her. Deep in the wilderness, miles and hours from any help, I feel protected and safe. I'm not scared of ghosts. In this moment, even Daniel is a friendly ghost. Fueled by the perfect September day, I wonder if maybe there's something we can do to save our marriage. Maybe it isn't over yet. Maybe there's hope.

Hand over hand, we climb a crack up the summit rock. The area smells vaguely of urine from all the people who have taken a pee break here. I sit down on the granite and take off my shoes, pressing my feet into the cool rock.

"You're a true genius for putting that together." I nod as Katie squeezes peanut butter mixed with Nutella into her mouth from a makeshift plastic tube. I refrain from joking about how similar it looks to the mud caked on my shoes.

"It's the best combo." She smiles through a sticky bite.

For a couple minutes we sit, eat, and stretch. I wiggle my toes back and forth and check for any reddish hot spots, places where my skin rubs awkwardly against my shoe and risks turning into a blister. But there are none; my mud-splattered feet are in great shape. Before I return them to their socks and shoes, I swipe away particles of dirt and sand that have become lodged between my toes.

In the distance, Santanoni Peak looms at 4,607 feet. The terrain goes up and down, and even though I know it's no more than three miles away, it looks as if it could be a day's journey through the dense, unrelenting forest. Katie and I gather our few belongings, and I hoist the thin straps of the daypack over my shoulders. As we scamper down the rock and duck back into the trees, I remind myself that mountain miles always look longer than they actually are. Break it down, one mile at a time, one hour at a time, one mountain at a time. All I need to do is take one step at a time— and let those steps add up. We're on pace and we are doing exactly what we need to do.

Katie and I retrace our route back through the bog to Times Square. At the web of intersecting trails, we take a sharp right past a large boulder and head south toward Santanoni. After a short descent, we hike quickly through a flat col, and I put my music back in for the sharp half-mile climb to the summit.

"Number seven!" I hold up seven digits and Katie snaps a picture next to the Santanoni sign. Of all the mountains this morning, Santanoni has the best view, and by now the fog has burned off from the valley so I can finally see the vast Adirondack wilderness around me. Voices float toward us, so we grab our buffs and put them over our nostrils and mouths. We scurry on, waving to the other hikers on our way back to Times Square. It's just after noon when we arrive back to our packs with three more High Peaks under our belt.

"Let's make our dinners so they can hydrate, and we can eat them throughout the day," I suggest.

Preparing dinner midday is a technique I've used on longer expeditions, when I'm moving most hours of the day. I have found it beneficial to get more calories in smaller portions during the day, rather than eating one big meal right before bed, especially when I only have six hours to digest it.

Katie gets the stove and fuel out of her pack. In a patch of sunlight, we arrange our muddy socks and shoes and give our pruney feet some time to breathe. This is our halftime. For the rest of the day, we'll carry our full packs for a dozen miles to the base of Allen Mountain.

"How are your feet doing?" I ask Katie, mindful of our self-care rules.

"Good, no hot spots. You?"

"Nothing to complain about." I fan my toes out to inspect them.

Katie passes me the cup of boiling water, and I pour it directly into the baggie of dehydrated shepherd's pie. While the food hydrates, I add caffeinated Tailwind to my water bottle. I will finish this 1.5 liters before 3 p.m. and not consume anything caffeinated afterward, so I can get my six hours of sleep tonight.

After some stretches, Katie and I begin the process of packing up. As much as we'd love to linger on the soft pine needles beside Bradley Pond, it won't be long before our bodies start to cool and our muscles stiffen. Socks and shoes go back on, and my feet readjust to their protective cages.

Once everything is packed, I swallow a few spoonfuls of shepherd's pie, then carefully rezip the heavy-duty ziplock bag and double-check it's sealed before stowing it at the top of my pack. Slowly, I cinch the cord to secure my precious calories.

"Ready?" I ask Katie through a mouthful of food.

"Yes, ma'am," she says.

"To Allen." I swing the pack onto my broad shoulders. The bear canister bumps against my spine, and I make a minor adjustment to my straps so it settles slightly to the side. With everything in place, Katie and I reconnect to the main trail and begin our long journey to the Central High Peaks.

Allen Mountain (4,340 ft.) — No. 8

MUCH OF THE mileage between the Santanoni Range and Allen Mountain is old logging roads. In this land of hunting camps and ghost towns, Katie and I pass an old stone furnace that was part of a nineteenth-century iron ore operation. Not far from where we are walking, Teddy Roosevelt stayed in a hunting camp. Roosevelt frequently visited the Adirondacks and was coming back from climbing Mount Marcy when he learned of the passing of President McKinley. It was around this very area he began his famous midnight ride to Buffalo to be sworn in as our twenty-sixth president.

There are two things about Teddy Roosevelt that have always resonated with me. First, he had severe asthma as a child but overcame it. Second, he healed through nature. When he was a young man, shortly after the birth of his first child, his wife and mother both died of unrelated illnesses on the same day. In his journal he wrote a large *X* along with the words, "The light has gone out of my life." He left his newborn daughter with his sister and went to the wilderness to grieve for three years. Ultimately, he believed it saved his life. That's why he was a major champion for the expansion of U.S. National Parks. He wanted others to have a chance to heal through nature. Of course, this didn't take into consideration the Indigenous peoples and settlers who were forcibly removed to "protect" the land and give exclusive access to white people.

But the modern world Roosevelt wanted to preserve wilderness as an escape from was nothing compared to what we have to escape now. Phones, computers, social media, the list goes on. When I was ten, I proclaimed that I didn't want a car; I wanted to walk everywhere or ride a horse. When cell phones and eventually social media arrived on the scene, I was immediately wary of adopting any new technology myself. Even now, Katie wears my expensive GPS watch, to save me from learning how to use it. I saw the effects of pervasive "tech" on my students in wilderness therapy, I became frightened for the young minds trapped in a world of technology overload and instant gratification. My dad told me that I was born in the wrong century. Often I felt invigorated by the way I chose to live my life, as close to the earth as could be; other times I was lonely. When I met Daniel, I was thrilled to find someone who cared as much about the environment as I did and wanted to live out of a backpack. It felt like a perfect match.

Blackberry bushes line both sides of the trail, and I maneuver my body carefully to avoid getting scratches. What Katie and I are doing—a fully human-powered expedition from one High Peak to another—is the quintessence of life and healing. Though some people balk at the idea of speed records and question whether nature can be properly enjoyed at such a pace, I cannot think of a more immersive experience. Every ounce of my being is here and now. I'm living in the woods. I smell musky and have scrapes on my forearms and dirt on my ankles. Hour by hour, I'm becoming more attuned with my surroundings. From the bushes, I pluck a few late season blackberries kissed by the sun and savor their seedy tartness. Through the twisted limbs of cedar trees, light refracts off the surface of Lake Sally, whose whiskey color comes from natural tannins leaching into the water.

Soon after we pass Lake Sally, the single track links up with a sandy two-lane road. Side by side we speed hike the flat terrain along the Opalescent River. Katie's legs open up and her pace is fierce; my trail runners pound the earth to stay with her. I don't need a GPS to tell me we've gone from a steady two miles per hour to four. We're approaching the line that turns hiking into running, and it's causing my toes to rub together in an awkward way.

After a few minutes of power hiking I suggest, "Let's slow down a little," afraid we'll pay for the enthusiastic pace later in the day.

Katie pulls it back to three miles per hour, but the friction between my toes continues to build, and I feel pieces of sand rub at the skin. I keep walking, thinking the coarse grains will eventually fall to the bottom of my shoe.

A mile later, we take a break on the bank of the Opalescent's clear waters. Even sitting down, there is uncomfortable pressure between the toes on my right foot, so I remove my shoe and sock.

"Oh, shit." A large bubble of fluid stares up at me from the inside of my big toe. The skin around it is red and inflamed. "Can I get some of your Leukotape?" I ask Katie.

"Sure."

Katie digs in her pack and tears off a strip of the aggressively sticky sports tape. I pry my other toe away, and Katie places a small Band-Aid on top of the blister and then wraps the beige Leukotape around it. Before putting my shoes back on, I knock them together, returning a dusting of mountain sand to the trail.

For the next quarter mile, I can't divert my focus from the hot pain of the blister. But then, as per the beauty of ultra distances, the pain is eventually replaced by a different pain—or at least, the mind moves on. For the next quarter mile, I notice my pack straps are biting at my collarbone. Then I knock my shin against a fallen log, and the pain shifts again. All the while, Katie and I move closer to Allen, closer to the end of our second day, sometimes acknowledging the ache aloud and sometimes ignoring it.

Around 4 p.m., we stop at the junction for the East River Trail. This is where we will leave our packs to pursue our final summit of the day. To our left, the Opalescent River flows over smooth stones, and I stare blankly into the cold water.

This is where Daniel laid me down, when my brain was on fire during my first thru-hike attempt back in 2012. Often in the years since, I have thought of this place. Every time the heat index creeps too high, and I feel the sweat roll down my body, I flash back to the plunge into the icy stream.

Standing now at the edge of the water, deep in the remote wilds, I recognize the significance of this place. Allen is a powerful and sacred mountain—in my eyes she is the gatekeeper of the thru-hike. If we make it to the summit of Allen, about fifty miles and eight High Peaks in, I know we've officially built a solid foundation for our quest. Every few years through the whispers of social media, I hear about attempts on the 46 speed records, both supported and unsupported. Allen is where a lot of them end. So perhaps she is the mystic who decides success or failure.

The approach to Allen, through lush hardwood forest with multiple stream crossings, makes this theory all the more believable. The hairs on my forearms prick upward.

"I think there are spirits in these woods." I peer over my shoulder into the dark undergrowth.

"Oh yeah?"

"Uh-huh, and they decide if we are worthy of the thru-hike or not."

"Interesting."

The rolling trail enters a patch of evergreen trees, and the earthy aroma is like a walking meditation to my senses. A small waterfall cascades to our left and the incline steepens. Cedar trees cling to the eroded embankment, their roots exposed. Before us, I catch patches of daylight, hints of the opening to the Allen slide.

"In 2012, I abandoned my attempt here, and in 2016, I came across a party evacuating a woman with a broken arm off the slide. She had slipped on the red slime." I point to a patch of gooey algae.

"Oh, that's horrible!" Katie gasps.

We pause for a moment on the slide, flexing our calf muscles against the steep rock and giving them some rest. Over the next brutal half mile, we will gain 1,000 vertical feet.

"The mountain did not give her blessing those years." I focus my attention on the views opening around me, instead of the lactic acid building in my legs, and hope Katie doesn't think I'm weird for sharing my mountain spirit theory.

After a moment, she sincerely adds, "Well, I hope Allen gives us a blessing today."

"Me too." I hit my thighs with closed fists to move the acid around, then begin to do a side step, shifting my feet into a horizontal position instead of a vertical one. This technique, often used in mountaineering, helps climbers ascend steep terrain with more stability. It also helps rotate which muscle groups are taking the brunt of the effort and unburden the strain of repetitive motion on the calves and thighs.

Katie and I fall into a prayerful silence as we ascend the open slide. I brush my hand over the soft bark of a cedar tree. Over my shoulder, the setting sun casts a flaming orange light into the trees around us, touching those seven peaks we have already climbed. Wisps of my blonde hair escape from my ponytail and glow like fire. The wind carries the sickly sweet scent of balsam. Goose bumps erupt on my forearms. I feel it. The blessing.

A brown sign with yellow letters announces our arrival to the sacred summit. We press our bodies together and smile for a quick selfie.

Just like on Seymour yesterday, we aim to get back down the steepest sections of the mountain before it gets too dark. We don our headlamps but give no rest to our tired legs. We have already covered a marathon's distance since leaving Duck Hole at 4 a.m. Packing up in the lean-to this morning is a distant memory. My sleepless night is like something from a past life.

Along the descent, Katie and I catch glimpses of the extinguishing sky. The once fiery hues soften to streaks of pink and purple as I drop down and scooch along the steepest parts.

Within a mile, safely down the slide, we reach easier terrain and our pace quickens, even though we are now navigating by headlamp.

"I'm not even tired!" I easily leap over a fallen log, still thinking about the beautiful sunset we just absorbed.

"How are you not tired?" Katie questions.

"I don't know, I guess when my body gets going, it wants to stay going. You know, physics."

"That's so Jan of you," Katie jokes.

In the delirium of moving for sixteen hours straight, Katie and I have decided that I am Jan and she is Cory, in tribute to the first team to complete the unsupported thru-hike. Jan is the taller of the two with a background in competitive sports, like me. And it's fitting because Jan and I personally know each other and are practically neighbors in Keene.

Katie related to Cory, because he dedicated the hike to someone important in his life who had passed away. Ed Bunk was Cory's mentor, and in 2002 Jim Kobak and Ed Bunk completed the thru-hike in ten days self-supported, meaning they had food caches along the way. It was Bunk's expedition that inspired Cory to take it to a whole other level: unsupported. No food caches. No aid. And dedicated to Bunk, who passed away in the beginning of 2009. "I must have read his trip report a dozen times," Katie told me when we first talked on the phone. Cory's detailed 2009 trip report was well known in the hiking community and something I had also studied closely.

The woods feel alive, the energy of past expeditions coursing through me. I imagine Cory and Jan walking this path, laying the groundwork for what was to come. Not many have come since, and still no women.

"Did you happen to bring any Benadryl?" I ask.

"Yeah, are you okay?" Katie replies.

"Um-hum, I think I'll need it to help me sleep tonight." My legs feel fresher than ever.

"That's wild." Katie laughs. "How do you still have energy on no sleep?"

"Genetics, I suppose."

From my dad's side of the family, I was blessed with long legs and an abundance of energy, which as a kid growing up, was easy to burn on the farm or playing sports. But sometimes I still got in trouble, going too fast on a four-wheeler or riding in the back of the speeding pickup, all for the thrill. In college, I struggled with so much downtime that boredom often led to impulsive and destructive behaviors. Like drinking too much before I was of legal age, which occasionally resulted in police involvement. Hiking long distances and working in wilderness therapy helped me put my energy to good use and understand how emotions were tied to behavior. Simply growing up and learning from my mistakes helped too.

In the darkness, we hear the stream that marks the junction and begin to search for our stashed packs.

"Over here." Katie spots them.

Swiftly, we distribute the gear of the daypack, strap into our packs, and pick our way across the stream. Our campsite for the night is only one mile away.

Since the sun set, the temperature has dropped significantly. We zoom across the last mile, energized by the brisk fall air.

"Here it is," I say, my headlamp catching a dark patch of flat trodden ground. "Our humble abode."

We shrug off our packs and set them by a fallen log that hugs the outskirt of the campsite. Then we set up our ultralight two-person tent, which we've borrowed from Tim Horvath, my mountain mentor and close family friend, who made a name for himself by climbing some of the highest peaks of the world, for nights we don't have access to a lean-to. The first time I set it up, I balked at the petite size and wondered if Katie and I could really fit in it together.

"Trust me, you'll want the body heat," Tim assured me.

Katie also packed a small tarp in case we ever needed to set up two shelters. But tonight we can see our breath, and suddenly the tent doesn't look as small as it once did. In the darkness, it actually looks cozy and snug. Katie arranges her gear first and puts her head toward one end of the tent. Then I arrange mine and put my head the opposite way, closer to the entrance, so we can maximize the space.

"Get some sleep tonight." Katie passes me a Benadryl.

I knock it back with a swig of bitter iodine-flavored water. "Thanks. You too."

For a few minutes, we rustle in our sleeping bags, trying to find the most comfortable position to spend the night. My blister throbs, now that there is little to distract me from the pain. When I try to lie on my back, the protruding bones along my spine press through my thin foam mat into the hard earth. I adjust my makeshift clothing pillow and exhale deeply, letting my face relax. Katie rolls over, and over again. Then like finding the last piece to a puzzle, our backs align and we settle into the earth. A breeze rustles the thin nylon exterior of our tent. For the next six hours, we sleep.

Day Three

September 12, 2020
32.4 miles
13,760 feet vertical gain

Lake Colden Campsite (2,764 ft.)

OUR ALARM SOUNDS at 4 a.m. From the warm cocoon of my sleeping bag, I stretch one hand to find my headlamp and click it on. A thin film of condensation coats the inside of our tent, a little oven of body heat in the cold morning. I want to sleep more, curled in the warmth of our den, but that isn't an option. We must pack up and get on trail as soon as possible. There is no snooze button out here. I rub the crust from the corners of my eyes and twist my body around on the ground. With movement comes the aches—a product of the fifty miles we've already covered.

Inside the restricted space of our sleeping bags, Katie and I change into our hiking clothes. I dig around for my sports bra and green polypro top from somewhere near my feet. Thankfully they have dried overnight. There is nothing less appealing than putting on a damp bra on a near-freezing morning. From my stuff sack pillow, I pull a hat, gloves, and fleece top.

I swing my legs to the entrance of the tiny tent and attempt to carefully peel the scrunched-up piece of Leukotape from my big toe. It resists, so I give it a swift tug and with it comes a large flap of skin.

"Ow," I squeal at the open flesh wound on the inside of my big toe. "Ah, this is so gross."

"What is it?" Katie asks.

"My toe. The blister popped, then I ripped off the loose skin."

"Oh no." Katie crawls over to examine my toe with her headlamp. "Wow, that's pretty big. Let me get some tape." She grabs the medical kit and gets to work, unfazed by the open wound. She places a square of moleskin, which has a circle cut out of the middle, on my toe, so it doesn't lie directly on the most raw area. Then she secures two fresh pieces of Leukotape around it.

"How does that feel?"

I wiggle my toes back and forth. The pressure of the binding takes away a lot of the pain.

"Great! Thanks, Nurse Katie." I smile appreciatively. "I'm not taking the tape off again until we're done with this thing."

I brush off the bottom of my feet before putting them in a pair of fresh socks and hope this is the only blister I'll acquire.

Outside the tent, stars twinkle through the canopy of maple and beech trees. A shiver ripples through my body, waking every nerve in every stiff muscle and joint. I hobble into the woods over low bushes and ferns to pee and retrieve our bear canisters.

A painful groan escapes my mouth as I squat, my quads protesting the uncomfortable position. My urine is clear in the beam of my headlamp, a good indicator I've stayed hydrated. After wiping with a maple leaf, I sanitize my hands and open my bear canister. I stuff a Clif bar into my pants pocket to warm it up. Ever since hearing about a fellow guide who broke his front tooth eating a frozen bar during a winter expedition, I use body heat to warm them up on near-freezing days. From the smallest tube of toothpaste I could find at the grocery store, I dab a little circle onto my travel toothbrush and brush my teeth until my mouth is full of foam. I spray my spit onto the forest floor, so it has the best chance of breaking down quickly and having a minimal impact on the plant life.

When I return to camp, Katie has all her gear out of the tent and packed up. She leaves for her trip to the bathroom while I crawl back into our sleeping space on my hands and knees to retrieve my sleeping bag and pack. Every item goes into the exact same space it came from; like a jigsaw puzzle, it only fits together if everything is where it belongs. I thoroughly enjoy the methodical rhythm of breaking down camp in the morning, even in the dark.

We disassemble the tent, and I give it a few solid flaps to knock off the moisture before storing it in my pack. Once everything is tucked in place, Katie and I pace around the campsite, making sure we have everything.

"Oh, the trekking poles." I grab them from the stump they're resting on. It would have been terrible to forget them. "Do you want to start with them?" I ask Katie.

"No, I'm good for now," she says.

"Okay." I adjust them to my height. "Just let me know when you want them."

Katie nods. Today will be our biggest day yet and a real test for us to stay on pace with the overall record. We'll be hiking the Adirondack Loj Loop—it consists of thirty-three miles with nine High Peaks and 13,000 feet of vertical gain. Fortunately, in a few miles, we will set up our camp for tonight, allowing us to make the loop with only the gear we need for the day.

I hike behind Katie along the Opalescent River toward Hanging Spear Falls. As we steadily gain elevation, I begin to shed my layers. First my gloves, then my hat. From my pocket, I take my Clif bar and check that it is pliable before biting down.

To the left, the thunderous roar of Hanging Spear Falls sounds in the darkness. Nearly one hundred feet in height with sheer drop-offs, its dangerous beauty lurks out of view. We ascend through the forest until a dawn light greets us at the Flowed Lands, a wide and shallow water area that was once dammed. Beside the remnants of the old dam, which was built in the 1800s, Katie and I pause to take a short break. For the first two days, our summits have been in small clusters with many miles between them. Now impressive ridgelines surround us. We are in the heart of the High Peaks.

Katie and I continue along the shores of the Flowed Lands until we reach the Lake Colden camping area. We cross a large wooden bridge, and I gaze across the water toward the domed massifs of Mount Colden and Algonquin Peak. Morning light touches their summits while the valley and lake remain in shadow. Across the bridge and back into a forest of balsam, we quietly search for an empty tent site. At 6:30 a.m., the campsite is a mix of hikers already up and out for their day hikes, those still snoring, and some just starting to stir.

"How about here?" I point to an empty area away from other campers, knowing we'll return to this campsite in the late hours of the night. We unclip from our packs and begin clearing marble-sized pebbles from our tent space.

"Let's try to be ready in ten minutes," I whisper. Today I feel the clock ticking more than ever.

My calves spring with energy as I move about, the soreness massaged out of them. Over the course of forty-eight hours and fifty miles, my body has become leaner and more muscular. My mind is sharper too, and I feed off the energy of the people around us, even if they are asleep. *This is where we all belong. Sleeping by rivers and lakes, with stars above and earth below. Our bodies get stronger the more time we spend out here.*

Unfortunately, Katie doesn't seem to be in the same flow state. She fumbles and trips, more frantic than efficient, trying to go as fast as she can. She feels the clock too, and the goliath of a day before us. I remember my nerves here four years ago, on my second attempt at the thru-hike. It was so intimidating to think about how I would feel by the end of it. Monstrous in miles and elevation gain, I had to break it down, focusing only on what was right in front of me, or it made me want to vomit.

"Hey, it's okay if we take a little longer," I say as we finish setting up our tent. "I'm going to go use the latrine."

Katie nods and continues to bustle about while I give her some space.

In 2016, I traveled the loop too lightly and ran out of calories when I was still six miles from camp. I also struggled with being alone and considered quitting at times, even though nothing was physically wrong. It surprised me that the mental component of being solo cut me so deeply. I wished I could be more solitary and take on huge multi-day, months-long endeavors like Heather Anderson, who set speed records on the Appalachian Trail and Pacific Coast Trail all by herself.

Back from the latrine, I sanitize my hands and finish packing. For the Loj Loop, Katie and I will be using our big packs, emptied of all camping gear. For the full day on trail, we'll need more space for food, headlamps, extra layers, and a medical kit than our small daypack would allow. We stash everything we won't need in the tent and set our bear canisters in the bushes on the outskirts of camp.

Katie's movements have stabilized, though I'm cautious about the intrusive thoughts that may be cycling through her mind. I know she is anxious about keeping up, but we're making great time.

I hope she knows everything out here is easier with her, and I am so grateful to be sharing this experience with a strong woman. Yesterday she was high when I was low. She got me through my doubts. I'm ready to return the favor.

Mount Marshall (4,380 ft.) — No. 9

KATIE SITS ON a log tying her shoe. "All set?"

"Yep." I clip into my pack, barely feeling the weight of my stripped down load. "You?"

"All good." She stands.

"Awesomesauce!" I put my pink sunglasses on the top of my head. "We got this, girl."

Katie follows me out of camp with a nod.

The trail snakes along the shores of Lake Colden, and morning light strikes the rocky, slide-strewn face of Mount Colden, which will be our last peak of the day. As we round the shoreline toward Cold Brook Pass, I scurry up a large wooden ladder affixed to a rock face, thankful for the backcountry trail crews who make this rugged terrain a little easier to navigate.

Early Adirondack trails were basically herd paths following waterways. During the 1930s, more trails were cut through the woods by the Civilian Conservation Corps (CCC) to provide jobs during the Depression. Today, the task falls on numerous trail crews, varying from paid professionals to volunteers, who work tirelessly to maintain and improve trail quality. But it's hard to keep up with the over 2,500 miles of trails within the Adirondack

Park. In the High Peaks Wilderness alone, there are close to three hundred miles of official trail, many of those are quite remote, and crews are not allowed to use chainsaws or power tools due to the 1964 Wilderness Act.

Once I clear the top of the ladder, Katie places her hands on the steps and begins to climb. I step forward, but then I hear a deep sickening *thunk*. Katie sucks in her breath. My stomach lurches. I whip around to see Katie in the middle of the ladder with her head resting against one of the steps.

"Shit, are you okay?"

Katie doesn't respond. The force that must have made that sound. Her inability to speak. This is bad. My breath catches in my throat until Katie moves again. She slowly ascends the ladder. At the top, her face is ghostly pale.

"I hit my knee really hard, and it felt like I was going to throw up for a minute."

"Ow." I grimace, relating to how Katie must have felt a week ago when she heard me smack my head against the fallen log. "It sounded awful."

I look at Katie's knee, which is hard to see under her pant leg, but there doesn't appear to be any blood or broken bones.

"I'm okay," she assures me, sucking in her breath.

As when a small child who has fallen off a swing looks to you to determine whether they should cry, I try to downplay my concern. "Okay. Well, let me know if it gets worse."

It feels a little insensitive, but I know from first-hand experience railing my body against objects in the backcountry that we'll know soon enough if it's a severe injury. Until then, we operate under the assumption that it's nothing more than a deep bruise and she will walk it off. Since we're within yelling distance of a Department of Environmental Conservation (DEC) caretaker cabin and helicopter pad, we don't need to make an urgent evacuation decision. Many rangers base out of this region too, because of the high number of rescues needed in this well-traveled area. Often those rescues are hikers who aren't fully prepared, but sometimes they're just unlucky and break their kneecaps on a ladder.

So, we keep hiking. Moderately at first, then I increase my pace back to our normal clip. Katie has no problem keeping up. My shoulders relax. Injury is lurking around every corner during an FKT attempt. In an unsupported team effort, if one person is injured and has to stop, the other's attempt becomes supported should they choose to continue. The supported records—both men's and women's—for the 46 are incredibly fast, coming in at three days and some change, mashing up the High Peaks in whatever order they find most efficient and driving between trailheads. If Katie drops out now, I wouldn't even have a chance at taking the supported record. Besides, it's not the style I yearn for. I want to carry all my gear from mountain to mountain. The thought of a third failed attempt makes me uneasy, and I try to replace it with logic. It's simple: If Katie goes down, I go with her. We move on together or not all.

"How's it feeling now?" I ask Katie as we climb Cold Brook Pass, about an hour after her knee struck the ladder.

"Better."

We both breathe more easily.

Soon we pass the skeleton of a Piper Cherokee 140 plane from a crash in 1969, which lies a hundred feet away from the trail. Originally painted white and blue, it's been decorated with yellow graffiti over the years. The pilot was caught in a downdraft and forced to crash-land in the pass between Mount Marshall and Iroquois Peak. Miraculously, he lived, but there was no way to get the plane back out of the crook in the mountains. Some hikers find the plane spooky, but I have the opposite feeling. The pilot was lucky to survive—I think the plane is a good omen.

By the time Katie and I reach the summit of Mount Marshall, it's 8:35 a.m. We've broken a sweat, and it seems the anxiety of the early morning has broken too. There's something about ascending two thousand feet over two miles that makes your brain discard all the extra garbage sucking energy from you. Somewhere in the sweat and the elevation gain, it becomes all about the movement.

On the summit of Marshall, I have two bars of service and send off a quick update to my group chat. *#9 Mount Marshall! Eight more to go for today.*

Words of encouragement ping in.

You got this!

Love you!

Looking at her phone, Katie adds with surprise, "Kenny says the fundraiser has reached over $2,000."

"Wow, that's amazing!"

At the end of our hike, our names will be listed as "unsupported" on the FKT website, but we are not alone out here. An audience is growing, and I can feel their love and support lift us high above the treeline.

Iroquois Peak (4,840 ft.) — No. 10
Algonquin Peak (5,114 ft.) — No. 11
Wright Peak (4,587 ft.) — No. 12

THE TRAIL CONNECTING Mount Marshall to Iroquois Peak is a herd path slicing around rock ledges that bypass an outcrop known as the Shepherd's Tooth. At first the herd path is easy to follow, but then it becomes more fragmented. Katie and I have to pause and eventually backtrack to where the vegetation is more trampled. Dense branches scratch against our arms, slowing our ascent. In 2022, after our hike, this path will be closed by the DEC to protect the fragile alpine environment on Iroquois Peak.

Finally above the treeline, Katie and I move from rock to rock, careful not to step on alpine vegetation and marveling at the dwarf shrubs and delicate white flowers that grow in near-freezing temperatures for two months of the year. I pull off my long-sleeve shirt and let it droop around my neck. My skin greedily soaks in the vitamin D. Iroquois will be our first summit with an unobstructed 360-degree view.

The mountain is named for the Indigenous peoples who lived in the Adirondacks long before it was a place of lumber and hunting camps. The name Iroquois was a derogatory term, meaning one who speaks with a forked tongue, aka "snake," given to them by the Algonquin people, who often fought against them. The name stuck in most textbooks, even though the Iroquois called themselves the Haudenosaunee, the "People of the Longhouse," and at the height of their influence extended east from New York State into the Ohio Valley and Lower Great Lakes Region and as far south as the Carolinas.

My hometown, Cherry Valley, New York, was a part of Iroquois nation and originally called Karatonga, "Land of the Oaks," by the Mohawk people. When my mother's ancestors, French Huguenot Protestants who sought refuge for religious freedom, arrived in the 1600s, their displacement began to displace others. They settled the Mohawk Valley and over time occupied the farmlands of the Haudenosaunee, which had once been ideal for farming corn, beans, and squash—the Three Sisters.

A part of me feels conflicted by what Katie and I are doing. Here we are, a pair of white women privileged enough to take a week off work, recreating on stolen land. The other part of me wants to recognize and honor what generations of women have had to overcome so that we might be allowed to chase this dream. That part of me wants to believe that like Kathrine Switzer, the first woman to run (illegally) in the Boston Marathon in 1967, our first for women will mean something to future generations.

At the summit of Iroquois Peak, I stretch my legs and look out at the land and waterways. It is certainly a privilege to be here.

"Here, let's look at where we were yesterday," I say, awkwardly holding up my cell phone to take a selfie, an art I'm not at all proficient in.

"Oh, I like that idea," Katie says.

We pose, resting our eyes on Mount Allen off to the south.

I check the photo. "Sweet, we're both in the frame!"

In the photo, sunlight hits our shoulders and the wind brushes a few strands of our ponytails across our smiling faces. We look strong, proud.

I think of all the summit photos of Daniel and me that have been collected since our first summer together in 2010. He'd taken so many in the early years but fewer and fewer as time went on. The last photo he took was in the fall of 2018; we had fingertips covered in peanut butter frosting at the top of Mount Haystack. Our heads leaned together in a moment of sweetness that had started to feel rare by then.

That was one of his passions—photography. Two years ago, almost to the exact day, we had come out to the High Peaks with a few family members who were working on becoming 46ers.

"It would mean a lot if you came," I'd told him. "They really want to see you."

My family loved Daniel and could feel his growing absence.

"It's Lauren's birthday and maybe you could bring your camera."

My cousin, Lauren, and Daniel had bonded over photography in the past. Early in our marriage, he'd show her a few professional tricks about cameras and time-lapse photography. He was always so talented at teaching.

"And we can celebrate your birthday too," I added.

"I don't know." He gazed down at his hands to avoid making eye contact.

"It will be fun," I promised, even though I had no idea if he'd be able to complete the eighteen-mile hike. He'd lost a lot of weight from his already thin frame and his pale Irish complexion appeared gray in certain lights. I could hardly remember the last time we'd been on a High Peak together. Maybe it was 2016 when he was capturing footage of me for the media outlets? That would've been two years before.

In the end, he packed his camera and came with us, stopping

to take a photo here and there. I had bought a dozen chocolate cupcakes from a local bakery and passed them out on the summit. From there we could see breathtaking views of Panther Gorge, Mount Marcy, the Great Range, and the valleys ablaze with turning leaves.

Daniel and Lauren took pictures, and for a few precious moments, it felt like the old days when everything still seemed possible. But that's the fallacy of summits, you can't stay there forever. Sooner or later, you must come down.

That was the last High Peak I hiked with Daniel.

Before we leave Iroquois, our tenth summit, I take a moment to trace our journey across the green blanket of forest from the Seward Range to Seymour to the Santanoni Range and Allen to Marshall. The skyline is rolling with long valleys between the ranges, nothing like the jagged peaks out west.

"On to Big Al," Katie says.

I smile at her fond nickname for Algonquin, her favorite High Peak, and the second highest mountain in New York. At over 5,000 feet, Algonquin is a fan favorite because of the spectacular views.

Small rocks placed by Summit Stewards outline patches of short grasses, which bow gently in the breeze. These stewards, usually recent college graduates with degrees in science or recreation, take their role protecting the alpine areas, through hiker education and structural guards like these, very seriously. To my right, the mountainside dips down to the dark waters of Avalanche Pass and Lake Colden. The Green Mountains of Vermont glimmer faintly under the eastern sunshine. Being above the treeline with panoramic views always reminds me of other mountainscapes I've traveled. The ten days I spent on the Nuumu Poyo, or the "People's Trail," in the High Sierra. The months I spent trekking in Nepal and climbing Aconcagua, the highest mountain in South America.

Katie follows the yellow splashes of paint and large rock cairns that mark the trail until she crests the round summit of Algonquin Peak. We both tap a foot against the circular geographic marker to make our summit official.

"How's your knee doing?" I check in again.

"Good, a little sore," she says. "Really not bad. Definitely going to have a good bruise."

I feel a deep sense of relief. Bruises can be managed—if it were going to flare up into something bigger, it should have happened by now. I grab my peanut butter and jelly wrap and eat it as we descend Algonquin, surrounded by mountains and blue skies. It doesn't get any better than this. A mile down, we come to the junction for Wright Peak and stash our packs in the woods, carrying nothing but the clothes on our back and one phone to snap a photo. The summit is only four-tenths of a mile from the junction.

Even though it's technically less than half a mile, the steep alpine terrain packs a punch, and Katie and I slow to stretch our calves. Algonquin rises to our right and Mount Colden's slides look like a monstrous bear swiped a paw down its face. As we approach Wright's rocky summit, Katie and I raise our buffs around our nostrils to share the view with a few other hikers who are all socially distanced from each other.

Out here, it's possible to forget about the pandemic for long stretches of time. But it's moments like these, when cloth clings to my mouth and moisture forms on my upper lip, that I remember all the fear and stress the pandemic has wrought on our lives. Katie and I debated if we should even attempt the FKT until things had calmed down. Even with the Canadian border closed, the number of hikers in the High Peaks is at an all-time high. Which means the number of rescues are too, and the last thing we want to do is tax an already overburdened system should something go wrong during our attempt. After a lot of debate, we decided we had a strong enough skill set to navigate most emergencies without help from professionals. If ever in doubt, we planned to play it safe.

Nye Mountain (3,895 ft.) — No. 13
Street Mountain (4,166 ft.) — No. 14

BY A LITTLE after 1 p.m., Katie and I have descended close to three thousand feet from the summit of Wright and set up our stove on the sandy shores of Heart Lake to boil water for our dinners. The shallow water ripples and glistens in the midday sun. From where we sit, we cannot see the heart-like shape it is named for.

Relaxing by the water's edge, I take off my shoes and socks to let my feet dry. They're in pretty good shape aside from the blister on my big toe, which I reinforce with another layer of Leukotape. The water boils and I carefully use my sock as a protective mitt to pour some of the liquid into a ziplock bag of shepherd's pie.

"Want some?" I walk with bare feet to deliver the pot of hot water to Katie. She briefly looks up from journaling on the back of one of the maps she is carrying. In preparation for the thru-hike, she designed one for each day, outlining our route and dissecting our mileage in detail, even annotating when we would have our packs and when we would leave them to pick up later. Half the page is already consumed by the words pouring from her pen. I'm impressed but also mildly concerned—we don't have an infinite amount of time at our disposal and she should be refueling.

"I don't want to forget anything," she explains, reading my facial expression.

"I get it." I soften my brow. In 2016, I carried a small Rite in the Rain weatherproof notebook on my solo attempt and jotted down notes at the end of each day, so I'd be able to write a detailed trip report like Cory had. This time around, I traded paper and pen for a cell phone to capture summit photos.

While our meals hydrate, I begin the process of putting my socks and shoes back on, making sure I get every little grain of sand off my skin. I glance over at Katie. We've already been off trail for twenty minutes, yet she continues to write.

"We better get going," I prompt.

Katie scribbles a few more words then tucks the paper away. She tries to zip her dehydrated meal and some of the water seeps out. She's rushing again, like this morning when we were setting up camp on Lake Colden.

"Hey, are you okay?" I ask, trying to ground her.

"Yeah." She shrugs. "I've never felt much connection to Street and Nye."

"Really?"

"Yeah, it's a long way out with no views," she says bluntly and shoulders her pack.

"Well, let's get these ten miles over with then." I laugh, surprised that a mountain lover like Katie could truly dislike two of the High Peaks so openly. "Do you want to take point? Or want me up front?"

"Why don't you lead for a bit, I think that would help," she says. "That way I can follow your shoes and zone out."

Katie steps quietly behind me. In 2016, I'd been battling myself in this very spot and trying to find motivation to continue. The Loj Loop is like a crown of mountains, up and down, up and down. The biggest challenge is the elevation gain and loss. Some of the nine summits are clustered in small groups without much ground gained and lost between, but there are five distinct climbs to tackle in the day. It will feel great to lie down tonight knowing we've checked so many peaks off the list. But there is something about this particular section right after midday that is extra draining.

I'm not worried though. Katie and I belong here. Not only do we belong, our bodies excel here. Women are built for endurance. Because we carry more fat on our bodies, it prevents our muscles from breaking down when we enter the zone of calorie deprivation. Our muscles are composed of more slow-twitching fibers, making them more endurance focused than men's, and our ability to multitask is proven to aid in high intensity, multi-day efforts. When Katie doubted her preparedness for the thru-hike, I gave her an issue of *Outside* magazine I'd been carrying around since 2017, themed "The Future of Adventure is Female." It highlighted women's capabilities at longer distances in a piece titled, "The Longer the Race, The Stronger We Get."

I feel it with every step through the hardwood forest. Halfway through our third day, my muscles are moving without complaint. The stiffness of the morning has worn off, and I feel the physical power I've trained all summer to employ. The herd path crosses a stream numerous times before the water peters out and the terrain steepens. My pace slows, so I can listen to Katie's breathing, a habit I've carried over from my days as a wilderness therapy instructor and guide. I know Katie's not my student or client, but I can't help feeling responsible for her out here. She's my teammate. I imagine she is observing me in similar ways without my knowledge.

The same way I observed Daniel two winters ago. He'd been struggling to keep a moderate pace on an easy hike. We hadn't been getting out much, but I hadn't realized how far gone the man who once ran up and down High Peaks with me was.

I'd smelled something then, fruity and sweet, but couldn't quite put my finger on it. After a while, I said to him, "Wow, you smell like alcohol."

"Oh, it's my new deodorant," he explained, between heavy breaths.

I hadn't thought much about it. We'd been growing apart—spending less time together. I couldn't even remember the last time we held each other or had sex. So not realizing that he had changed products, and the way he smelled, without me knowing felt plausible. And sad.

The terrain flattens and the trail splits. At the junction, we drop our packs, take a right, and climb a short distance through dense, unbroken pine forest to the sign marking the summit of Nye Mountain. If there wasn't a sign there, we might not even know we were at the top, surrounded by trees on all sides. Grateful to have made it this far in the journey, I tag the sign with my hand. Katie snaps a photo. We retrace our path back to the junction and complete the half-mile trek to the top of Street Mountain, which is similarly treed in.

"Ah, it feels so good to get these two done." Katie exhales on the summit. "I've been dreading them all day."

"Alright, show the camera how much you love Street." I click a photo of Katie by the summit sign.

She laughs and grins widely. In good spirits and with a quicker pace, we begin our four-mile descent back to the Adirondack Loj.

"Hey, I gotta pee," I call to Katie half a mile away from the lodge. I want to squat and do my business before we're back in the mix of heavy hiker traffic.

"Okay." Katie continues down the trail to give me some privacy.

Off trail, I peel down my pants and underwear and instantly recognize the sweet, copper scent of blood.

"There you are," I say.

Katie and I had talked about our cycles when we planned the thru-hike. Ideally, we would have found a window where neither of us would have it, but our cycles were two weeks apart. So that meant one of us would likely experience the beginning or the end of a period on trail. Because we wanted to avoid the crowds of Labor Day weekend and wait for the humidity to break, it landed on mine. I didn't mind. During a normal period, when I'm not trying to backpack 180 miles in one week, the worst symptom I have is lower back pain on the first day. Today, on day three of the thru-hike, I am unable to differentiate period pain from hiking pain.

While crouching, I dig into my pack and grab a heavy-duty pad. I stick the adhesive backing of the pad to the inside of my underwear and yank my pants back up, wiggling to accommodate the extra material between my legs. I've never minded pads, especially after learning what a tampon put in place by dirty fingernails can do. Plus, I revel in the idea of giving my blood back to the earth, seeing it drip on the leaves when I stop to pee.

"Got my period," I announce when I rejoin Katie on the trail.

"Oh no," Katie commiserates, misunderstanding my tone.

"No, it's all good," I assure her. "I am woman. Bleeding while setting a record. Badass."

The follicular phase, or the first two weeks of the cycle, is when hormones are lowest and energy is highest. This includes when we are bleeding, and it is actually the best time to go for an endurance effort. Periods are just another variable to factor in as an athlete. As I have learned more about the processes in my body, I have become better able to harness their power and not be knocked down by the stories we are told.

Throughout history and still to this day, women have been excluded from mountain expeditions because of their menstrual cycles and outright sexist societal views. When I traveled to Nepal and India, I saw that in certain villages, women were kept out of schools and places of worship while menstruating. During puberty, many girls fall so far behind in classwork they are forced to drop out. They don't know their periods make them stronger, more energized, no less equipped to learn or participate in school.

Thinking about the injustices of being in a female body gives me a second wind. Katie and I are completing a route no woman has done before, pushing our legs up and over rugged mountains to prove we are capable. More than capable—we are built for this. And for at least part of this journey, my body is expressing its womanhood by bleeding between these powerful legs. This story will stand in direct opposition to those stories. By living it, and telling it, we invite others to see what we are truly capable of. And hopefully push the door of opportunity open a little wider for women and girls around the world.

Phelps Mountain (4,161 ft.) — No. 15
Tabletop Mountain (4,427 ft.) — No. 16

I'M NOT THE only one with a second wind. Katie speeds over the relatively flat terrain past the Adirondack Loj parking area and toward Marcy Dam. I draft behind her momentum.

At almost 5 p.m., day hikers are returning to their cars. They walk their dogs toward the parking lot, laughing and making plans for post-summit beers and burgers. It's the most people we've seen in days. I can smell the chemical odor of their colognes and perfumes—abrasive against the scents of nature, which have filled our nostrils for days.

The day hikers' energy gives us more energy. I envision us crossing our finish line, still a hundred miles and several days away. I think about what my first meal at home might be. Maybe a burger and sweet potato fries. Maybe a pizza.

"It's not a matter of if we finish!" I cheer, raising my trekking poles above my head and sashaying my hips side to side. "It's when!"

Katie follows my antics, and a mile later we arrive at the large boulder that marks the junction for Phelps.

"Let's make it to the summit for sunset," Katie suggests.

An ambitious plan to get us up the final mile, which ascends approximately two thousand feet in less than forty-five minutes.

Confidently, Katie begins picking her way up the rocky trail in silence. Our agreements become more and more important as the miles and summits stack up. We fall into rhythmic movement as a pair. Behind her, I focus on my breathing and making each step as efficient as possible. *Pick your line, pick your line,* I tell myself over and over. My calves tighten in response to the ever-steepening trail. I pause to stretch them against the wide trunk of a balsam tree. Piney sap sticks to my palm as I pull myself into a deeper stretch.

To conserve energy, I put my head down and follow Katie's feet. She can pick the line for both of us. In the final quarter mile before the summit, small slides carve through the forest, opening views beyond the trees. Between the summits of Colden and Algonquin, the western sky is a stratification of pink and purple hues.

"Oh my God, this is too beautiful," I gasp, turning my head every few minutes to gaze upon the changing sky. It's a bold goal, but we're going to make it to the top of Phelps Mountain in time for a show.

On the summit rock, Katie lays the 46Climbs bandana next to the marker and looks off into the sunset.

Quietly, I retrieve the headlamp from my pack and affix it to my forehead. I squeeze Katie's shoulder. After a moment of silence for all those lost to suicide, we begin our descent. I think of Daniel as the light fades from the sky. I'm worried about him. It's a feeling I know well. I've spent years worrying about him: trying to decipher what he is thinking and feeling behind the illusion of "okayness" he presents.

A couple of months before we hiked Haystack for my cousin's birthday, I knew something was very wrong. But I struggled to make sense of it. He didn't eat. He didn't sleep. I was always coming up with ideas to try and help, but nothing seemed to break through. The meditation corner, the plants in the living room, the journaling. He wasted away, growing smaller and paler and sicker. One day, I looked over at him sitting on the couch and imagined putting my fist through his chest. Like punching through tissue paper, it would go right through. He wasn't even there. He was a ghost. His anxiety spread, filling up spaces in the house, wrapping its fingers around my neck. Sleep was the only reprieve from my daily headaches. I began taking extra melatonin at night to secure those ten peaceful hours. I was scared I was becoming a ghost too.

Sometimes I took long trips to my parent's house in Cherry Valley to recharge.

"Something is wrong," I finally told my mother on one of those visits. Out of all the people in my life, she knew the most about our marriage. But I didn't know how to explain the feeling I had.

"Well, marriage is hard." She moved about the kitchen, layering ham and cheese on bread.

It was a stifling hot July day. I lay on the dining room floor, staring up at the ceiling fan twirling above me. A dizzying ring. A vow. A cage.

"I know marriage is hard." I pushed myself to a sitting position and glared at her. "But this is different, and I can't figure it out."

"I think sometimes you want too much," she said.

Like me, my mother was emotionally exhausted. She'd been taking care of her parents, watching her mother lose mobility and always being there to take up the slack.

"What do you mean?" I asked.

"Well, you travel, you climb mountains, you write. I think it's hard to keep up with you."

"But, but . . ." I stammered. "That's who I've always been and that's who he used to be too. That's what our life was supposed to be." My voice trailed off, lost between quivering lips.

Daniel and I had gotten engaged in a lean-to. We wrote our

wedding invitations on birch bark. We worked as wilderness therapy instructors together and made each other Christmas and birthday gifts with our own hands. The vows we made deep in the mountains mattered to me, and I felt like I was dying in order to uphold them. I wanted to be married. I wanted to go through joys and sorrows together. I wanted to fight and grow. Never did I not understand that marriage would be hard. But how could I have a marriage without a husband?

Suddenly I hurt in a deep place and felt ill. *Was this all my family and the world saw? That I was growing distant from Daniel because I was too ambitious and wanted to be a climber and a writer?* I wanted to scream. Tears escaped from my eyes and ran down the side of my face. Our marriage was dying, and I couldn't figure out how to stop the bleed.

The phone rang.

"Hello?" My mother said in between bites of her sandwich. I could hear the tone of my grandfather's voice through the speaker pressed to her ear.

"Um, hum. I'll send Bethany up to help and then I'll be up." She returned the phone to the charger. Turning to me, my mother said. "Grandma fell, she's on the floor." She used the same matter of fact tone she would with a patient at work. "Get her to the couch and get her something to eat and drink. I'll be up shortly."

I pushed myself off the floor and swiped my fingers under my eyes to erase the tears. I would put my emotions away for now and do what needed to be done, just as my mother had taught me, just as her mother, who now needed to be lifted off the floor of her own house by her granddaughter, had taught her. It was a cycle of self-reliance. A blessing and a curse.

When I arrived, my grandmother lay on her side on the kitchen floor with my grandfather standing beside her. At eighty, his own body was too physically limited to do anything to help her. His hands rose to hide his face, scrunched with tears. Grandma cried too. I stood frozen for a long moment, just letting the tears fall and aching in shared sadness. They were like second parents to me. I had grown up in this house, with my sisters and cousins, crawling all over the very floor my grandma could not get up from. I dropped to my knees and helped her to a sitting position.

"Alright grandma, let's get you to the couch," I said. "I'm going to lift you."

"Oh, be careful of your back," she said, always worried about everyone else.

"I'm strong." I smiled and sucked the snot back into my nose. "You know I'm a mountain climber, right?"

"Oh yes. I know, I know you are very strong."

"Okay then, here we go." I reached my arms under her frail body. She clung to my neck as I carried her to the couch and set her down gently. I stuffed a pillow behind her back, so that she could sit up and drink a bottle of strawberry-flavored Ensure through a straw.

Twenty-two years ago it had been *her* setting *me* gently on the couch with a pillow under my broken foot to wait for my mother to arrive. I'd been fooling around in the machine shed while my grandmother backed up the small tractor, and got my foot caught underneath the wagon.

When my mother came to take me to the hospital, my grandmother was a nervous wreck.

"It's not your fault mom," my mother told her. Then she looked at me pointedly, "Come on."

"But, it hurts," I whimpered.

"Bethany, we have to go to the hospital. Your foot is broken and you need a cast." My mother's clear and matter of fact tone said it all. *You are here because of your actions.*

It wasn't like that now. My grandmother had done nothing

wrong. Only worked hard all her life, passed her strength down to my mother and to me, and now, grown old like we all will someday, God willing.

Next to the couch was a window that faced north and through the haziness of the day, we could both see the Adirondacks.

"Those are your mountains." She pointed.

"They are."

"Whenever I see them, I say there's my Bethany." Her blue eyes lit up and my lower lip quivered at the genuine happiness that came from thinking of a grandchild. On the couch I sat and I rubbed my grandmother's feet until I saw my mother's van come down the driveway, just like I had so many times as a child.

"She lifted me like a feather," my grandma reported as soon as my mother entered the living room.

"She's strong." My mother hugged me, her energy softer than before.

"I'll go check the veggie stand," I said, giving my grandparents each a kiss on the cheek and space to be with my mother. Alone in the small wooden building that held the produce my grandfather picked from the gardens every morning, tears kept falling to the concrete floor while I restocked the potatoes and corn. I thought of my grandparents' bodies and my husband's mind both slowly breaking down, and began to realize that loss comes in many forms.

I wanted a marriage. I wanted Daniel. I wanted it to be hard and to grow old with him. If I fell when I was an old woman and couldn't get back up, I wanted him to be there next to me. I just didn't know if we could get there together.

In the darkness, my trail runner collides with a rock, causing my body to lurch forward.

"Ow." I catch myself with my trekking poles.

In the distance, a headlight bobs.

"Howdy!" A man's voice calls.

"Hi there," Katie and I call back as we step to the side of the trail for him to pass.

"Where ya'll heading?" he asks.

"Oh, Tabletop," I say. Most people would think we were nuts if we took the time to explain what we were doing. Often, especially at the end of a long day, it's easier to say little, put our heads down, and keep moving.

"Well, enjoy your hike." He hobbles past us, adding with a laugh, "I did Marcy today and boy am I hurting."

"Safe journeys out!" I wait for him to get a few paces down trail from us and out of earshot before joking to Katie, "Probably would hurt his feelings if he knew what we did today."

"Yeah, especially if he knew where your minivan is parked."

As we weave through the mud at the beginning of the herd path to Tabletop, the light of my headlamp grows dimmer. I click through all the setting options, each as weak and fluttering as the last, confirming my suspicion that my batteries need to be replaced. I'd planned to get to day four or five with the first set of batteries. Between the two of us, Katie and I have only packed six spare triple-A batteries, one set for each headlamp. I hold off from changing them out until we reach the treed-in summit of Tabletop, our eighth peak for the day. One more to go.

"Hey Katie, can you shine your light over here?" I ask, crouching over my pack. "I have to change out my batteries."

"Uh-huh." Katie leans over me.

I switch out the old batteries with my fresh set. I turn the light on to the lowest setting and place it back on my head. Perhaps I should've upgraded my headlamp before this adventure. Little good that realization does me now as we head down the mountain. In front of me, I hear Katie's shoes scuffing against the ground;

she's not picking up her feet and her pace is slowing. The day is starting to catch up with us.

Mount Colden (4,715 ft.) — No. 17

"Let's get some water." I stop at the river crossing by Indian Falls. On the bank of the stream is a large rock where we remove our packs to sit. I absorb the sound of the falls to my right while monitoring Katie. Out here in the darkness, we are each other's lifelines and it's both our jobs to take care of each other. Just like she led us on day two, I'm leading us to the end of day three. It's a baton we pass back and forth.

I stare into the nothingness of Indian Falls. In daylight the water cresting over rock foregrounds a perfectly framed view of the MacIntyre Range. Under the blanket of night, it's like it doesn't exist at all.

"We have to keep drinking and eating," I say, referencing our rules of self-care.

Katie nods.

We open the dinners we made at Heart Lake and eat in silence. The saltiness tastes good. In between bites of my shepherd's pie, I refill our water bottles and drop them with iodine. As I crouch between the rock and water, my legs throb with fatigue. *One more mountain*, I tell myself. *And we have to go over it to get to our camp. Our tent. Our bear canisters. Where everything is already set up and ready for bed. We just have to get there.*

Sitting again, I stretch my legs and think of my sleeping bag, laid over my ground pad, patiently awaiting my return. The bottoms of my feet pulsate. I fantasize about the moment I'll be able to unlace my shoes and toss them outside the tent.

"Ah, I needed that." Katie finally speaks again, only after her dinner is completely gone.

"Me too," I agree.

"I think I pushed too hard going up Phelps for sunset and didn't drink enough."

"I'm guilty of that too," I say, thinking of how energized I felt passing through the lodge area. "Especially when we're in a flow state, we need to make sure we keep fueling so we don't crash."

"I was definitely crashing coming off of Tabletop," Katie reflects. "And I wanted to keep going to get this day over with."

I can instantly recall numerous times I pushed myself too hard, forgoing a much-needed break only to learn I would have gone farther and faster had I stopped to rest. Katie and I both know this, but it's one of those lessons we must learn time and again. Under the pressure of performance, even the most experienced athletes can falter.

"Do you mind taking point on Colden, so I can follow your feet again?"

"Not at all." I push myself from the rock. "We got this. And here, take the trekking poles. They will help you." I pass the poles to Katie and she accepts them.

Across the stream, we veer down a connecting path that brings us to the Lake Arnold Trail.

"Just follow my feet. Don't think about anything else," I remind Katie when the approach to Mount Colden steepens. Every now and then I stop to make us eat and drink. As we make our way up the mountain, pine trees become more prevalent, and the forest falls another shade darker. We pass over the false summit, catching a full sky of stars and a warm wind blowing in from the west.

Forty minutes before midnight, we stand on the summit of Colden. To the east, the lights of Lake Placid twinkle blue, yellow, and red. Every other direction is a black abyss. The stars shine brightly overhead, and I gaze up to the constellations, fixing my eyes on the Big Dipper, Cassiopeia, and Orion. I look toward Lake Colden, somewhere in the darkness, where our tent and sleeping bags wait for our return.

I'm extra cautious as I guide us down the sheer rock faces by way of multiple ladders and staircases. Though we are both anxious to get down the mountain and be done for the day, we must take care in this area, where a single misstep could result in a serious injury. Midnight comes and goes, and it feels like we're still miles from camp. Every step forward feels like purgatory. I want to talk to Katie to pass the time, but it feels like too much effort. My mouth is dry.

"This sucks," I whimper.

I'm bonking.

We've been up and on the move for twenty-plus hours. I can feel the warmth of blood between my legs. The day has taken a few hours longer than expected and we don't stumble into camp until almost one in the morning.

"Thank God, there it is," I whisper, so as not to wake the other campers. If they weren't around, I would fall to my knees and scream with joy.

"I've never been so happy to see a tent," Katie agrees.

Operating purely on autopilot, we retrieve our bear canisters, brush our teeth, and stash our food. To pee, I brace my body against a tree. Drops of blood, a little bit of life force, fall as an offering to the mountains for getting us safely through the Loj Loop.

In the tent, Katie and I change our clothes, wipe our feet, and crawl into our sleeping bags. I set my alarm for 6:30 a.m., pushing back our wake-up time to keep us to our six-hour sleep rule and let our bodies recover. We exchange good nights and Katie drifts off to sleep, snoring lightly. On my back, I look at the ceiling of our tent. It's early Sunday morning. The last time I checked the weather report, on Thursday before we left my house in Keene, it predicted a forty percent chance of stormy weather this afternoon. I had waffled about gear, and decided in the end not to pack rain pants. I wonder what has happened to the forecasted storm. Have rain chances increased or decreased? Is it still coming at all?

"Please don't rain, please don't rain," I pray to the skies above me. When the alarm sounds tomorrow, we'll be gearing up for the thru-hike's most technical and exposed terrain. A storm above the treeline could easily knock us off record pace.

Day Four

September 13, 2020
15 miles
7,530 feet vertical gain

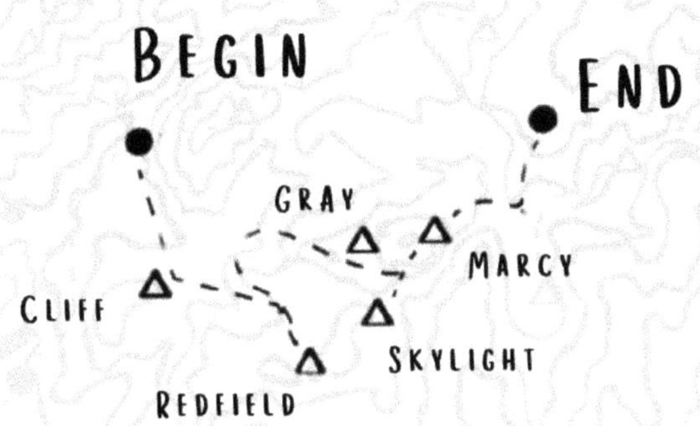

Cliff Mountain (3,960 ft.) — No. 18
Mount Redfield (4,606 ft.) — No. 19

I CRAWL OUT of the tent to study the somber gray sky, wondering if it will turn into a storm. Rain will make everything we're trying to accomplish harder. But right now, I'm thankful for a dry start to our day. At least I don't have to stuff a wet tent into my pack.

"I'll get the bear canisters," Katie offers, our communication boiled down to a science. Never saying more than we need, conserving energy on all fronts.

"I'll break down the tent."

My body aches as I bend to pull stakes from the earth and fold the nylon fabric. Most of the stiffness congregates in my back. My arms and hands are decorated with red scratches, and my blue nail polish is chipped. My hiking clothes are crusted with sweat and dirt, so I put off changing into them as long as I possibly can. Moving about in my polypro bottoms and fleece top, I notice my sleep clothes are getting a little rancid too. One baby wipe a day is no match for either my armpits or Katie's. We are musky like the wild animals who live in these woods. I'm thankful to spend most of our hours in the open air, versus zipped up in a tent with our own stink.

Katie returns with our bear canisters. I open mine, taking out a Clif bar and Tailwind packet for breakfast. I'm not hungry, but I have to keep putting calories in like clockwork. Mindlessly, I stuff a piece of bar into my mouth and pull my stiff sports bra on over my fleece top, before maneuvering my arms out of the long-sleeves and pulling it from under the bra, never revealing myself to any camper who may happen to wake up and poke their head out of their tent. I sit on a log to shimmy out of my black polypro leggings. Cuts and bruises color my sun-deprived legs. Purple and green bull's-eyes mark where my body has connected with an army of sticks. I slide each leg through my dusty pants and tie the drawstring around my thinning waistline. Finally, I shake out yesterday's socks and lace up my La Sportivas.

We trek out of camp and rock hop across the low, clear waters of the Opalescent River. The mouth of the river is wide and I pause multiple times, thinking about my next move like a video game.

"Want to start with the trekking poles?" I ask Katie once we're safely across.

"Yes, please." She eagerly extends her right arm to take them. "I'm so glad you brought these; they saved my legs on Colden last night. I'm officially converted." The carbide tips of the poles tick against the rock as Katie picks her way along the sandy banks of the Opalescent.

For a mile and a half, the trail winds gradually uphill along the river. Our bodies warm among the cedar trees, whose roots cling fiercely to whatever shallow soil they can find. As the trail steepens, a series of sheer drops and waterfalls separate us from the river, which grows more rapid and wild below.

The trail veers away from the river and I glance to my left, looking for signs of Uphill Lean-to. This is where Katie and I will stash our packs for the out-and-back to Cliff Mountain and Mount Redfield. Finally, the campsites come into view, followed by the circular logs of the lean-to, which is conveniently unoccupied. Inside, we drop our packs to pull out the few items we'll need for the next two summits. I can already feel his presence.

His writing is still there. I know it is, but I don't look up. I don't want to see it. Ten years ago, this is where Daniel and I got engaged on a frosty November morning. Curled into our sleeping bags, I felt two things bursting from me. One, I wanted to marry this man and go on adventures with him until our time on earth was through. And two, a large boil-like pimple protruding from my chin. The latter made me second-guess acting on the former. I thought it might be better to wait until I felt a bit more glamorous with a covering of makeup. But I'd never been good at waiting, and I knew Daniel wasn't the type to care about that kind of vanity.

"I want to marry you," I said, the words tumbling from my mouth.

Daniel looked up from his journaling, a crescent-moon grin spreading across his face. "Well, I want to marry you too."

"Then let's get married," I said before pouncing on him, still wrapped in my sleeping bag. We laughed and kissed, fumbling to get our hands free so we could hug each other. Over a breakfast of peanut butter and granola, we debated if we should write our piece of history on the lean-to. Countless names were etched above and around us, mere mortals trying to leave their mark on a certain time and place. Some more authentic and mature than others, even though all of it was illegal. You could get a ticket from the DEC for defacing a lean-to.

"How about very lightly in pencil?" Daniel suggested.

I agreed.

With his sleeping bag wrapped around his shoulders, Daniel penciled into the top beam in all-capital letters: "And there we were, in a lean-to my father built when I was a child, when she asked me to marry her and I said yes."

Everything about the moment felt right. The cold morning. Lying in a lean-to nestled in the heart of the High Peaks. Daniel loved me for who I was. My ambition, my passion, my drive and ability to run toward what I wanted instead of being stopped by fear or insecurity. And I loved him for who he was. Every piece of him, even the pieces he viewed as imperfect and flawed.

I glance up at the ceiling beam. I can't help myself. There it is, Daniel's all-too-familiar capital handwriting, same as on the note I left behind only a few days ago. It's faint, the words barely visible, slowly wearing away with time and the elements. Maybe he should have written in something bolder, more permanent. Within a few years, I doubt the words will be legible at all.

"This is where Daniel and I got engaged," I tell Katie, feeling a sentimental need to honor that moment and all the times Daniel was there for me.

"Ah, what a perfect place." She smiles.

"It was." I stash my pack in the back of the lean-to, exactly where Daniel had lain when I told him I wanted to be his wife. For just a moment, I long to be twenty-four again. And I want Daniel to be there with me.

Katie and I hike away from the lean-to, and as the trail to Cliff Mountain steepens, thoughts of breathing and foot placement replace memories of Daniel. My body bends forward as we navigate the rock scrambles. Having a bit of rock-climbing experience certainly helps as Katie and I pick the most direct lines up the layered cliffs. The trail flattens before continuing through a swampy section. We delicately balance on logs to avoid falling knee-deep into pigpen-like muck. We giggle and laugh, energy pouring from us, miraculously healed by six hours of rest. The strenuous Loj Loop seems like it happened weeks ago.

"I feel great!" Katie taps the wooden sign for Cliff, which is nailed to a haggard pine tree. Just after 8 a.m., we're moving at an efficient pace.

"Me too," I say.

Our bodies and minds have begun to accept the rhythm of the trail. We leave Cliff and reach the summit of Redfield an hour and a half later, covering the two and a half miles with relative ease.

Next to the summit tree, I sit and take a few sips of Tailwind.

"I wonder how Lyle is doing," Katie reminisces with a chuckle.

Four weeks ago in this very spot, we were finishing our four day get-to-know-each-other scouting mission when we stumbled upon a distressed hiker. We had already summited six High Peaks in the cold rain that day—twenty miles with full packs on—before arriving at Uphill Lean-to and promptly falling asleep.

It was almost 11 p.m. when I heard a voice cry out over the sounds of rain dripping from the roof.

"Help!" The voice cried louder.

I nudged Katie's shoulder, shaking her awake. "Katie, someone is calling."

"Huh?"

"There's someone calling for help."

Within five minutes, we had donned our headlamps and damp hiking clothes and devised a plan. Shivering against the cool night, I laced up my shoes and grabbed some calories from the bear canisters, for the lost hiker and ourselves. Out on the main trail, we splashed through puddles of rainwater, feeling the icy water surge into our already wet shoes and soak our feet. We stopped every few seconds, put our heads down, and listened. Gradually, my body warmed from the movement and intensity of the moment.

"Hello?" We called in unison, our voices booming out into the pitch-black night.

We paced up and down the trail waiting for a reply. We were just about to return to the lean-to when we heard the voice again.

"Help!"

They were close. We backtracked a few paces.

"Hello!" Katie and I yelled.

"Hello!" The voice responded.

My body instinctually shifted from search mode to assessment mode after all my wilderness training. *In what kind of condition would we find them? Were they hurt? Hypothermic?* We pushed our way through thick brush away from the trail. To our left, Uphill Falls Brook acted as a navigational tool to help us keep our sense of direction. My headlamp shone through the forest shadows before reflecting off something white and shiny. An exposed belly. I raised my light up his large torso and flashed him in the face by accident. He staggered backward, putting up a hand to block the light. Rain pants stuck to his legs and sagged low below his belly. On his feet were a pair of Adidas slides.

"Hey." I turned my headlamp to the side of my head, "Sorry about that. What's your name?"

"Lyle," he slurred, his eyes glassy and his complexion a sickly pale color.

"Do you know where you are?"

"No. I sent out a Spot page." He pointed to the red blinking light on the device attached to his external frame pack. Like any well-trained first responders, Katie and I surveyed the scene and found his pack, which was saturated with mud and water. As were the layers of clothing he'd stripped off and thrown to the side. He didn't seem fully conscious—I guessed 50 percent at best—and his lips were purple. Most likely he'd been cold and wet for most of the day and was now in the early stages of hypothermia, even though it was only August.

"My name's Bethany, and this is Katie." I spoke slowly and deliberately, as if he were a kindergartner, knowing his mind wasn't firing on all cylinders. "We're gonna help you out. There's a lean-to nearby, and we'll get you some food and help you dry your gear."

Lyle nodded but didn't speak.

Katie and I led him back through the brush toward the trail. We asked him simple questions, trying to gather as much information as possible. The day before, Lyle had come in with a group of friends, partied at Marcy Dam, then set off for Mount Marcy via Lake Tear of the Clouds. Without proper footwear, his pace had been too slow, so his friends left him with the Spot pager and continued to the summit. Trying to backtrack to Marcy Dam, he'd taken a wrong turn and lost the trail along the swollen river.

When we arrived at the lean-to, I set up my one-person tent and Katie made Lyle a bed out of her tarp. We'd each packed a shelter in case the lean-to was full. We didn't have any clothes that would fit his linebacker frame, so we encouraged him to get in the tent and burrito wrap himself in the tarp.

He crawled into the tent but then poked his head back out. "Do you guys wanna smoke? I have some weed."

"No thanks, Lyle. It's time for bed," I had said, secretly impressed he'd managed to keep one thing dry.

He nodded, zipped up the tent, and within a few minutes was snoring.

"We should let someone know we found him," Katie whispered. "So they can call off the search team."

Seven miles into the backcountry, our two closest options for contacting the DEC, which handles emergencies throughout the Adirondacks, were to either drop down to the caretaker cabin on Lake Colden (about a five-mile round trip) and notify the on-call caretaker or climb to the top of Mount Redfield (about a three-mile round trip), where there was enough cell service to get a call out.

"How about going back up Redfield?" I suggested and Katie agreed.

Though well after midnight we restocked our packs with food, water, and emergency gear to hike back up Mount Redfield, which we had climbed only six hours before. On the summit, Katie talked to a DEC dispatcher and arranged for the Lake Colden caretaker to hike to the lean-to in the morning and assess Lyle. By the time we shimmied back into our sleeping bags, assured Lyle would be taken care of, it was past 3 a.m.

On the riverbank, near where we found Lyle soaked and shirtless, Katie and I stop to refill our empty water bottles. Orange birch leaves float at the edges of the current, hinting at fall's arrival. The sky is still overcast, but not a single drop of rain has fallen.

"You know, that day of the rescue was when I really knew," I say to Katie.

"Knew what?"

"That we could do the thru-hike together."

The moment had spoken to our strengths as a team. And our values. If something went wrong, I knew we would be able to come up with a plan and execute it. Even if we were tired after a long day, even in the cold and dark with wet feet. If someone needed to be rescued, Katie and I would do it. Abandoning our FKT effort wouldn't even be discussed. That's just who we were.

"That was the moment for me too." Katie caps her water bottle.

"Thank you for doing this with me," I say. It's hard to express the depth of my gratitude to Katie. She had been the one to reach out and rekindle a fire in me. She was the reason we were out here together, putting me on the cusp of completing a decade-long dream.

Gray Peak (4,840 ft.) — No. 20
Mount Skylight (4,926 ft.) — No. 21

Slowly, Katie and I begin the long slog up to Lake Tear of the Clouds, the source of the Hudson River, which lies between the shoulders of Mount Marcy and Gray Peak. We readjust to moving under the weight of full packs. Thankfully, they have grown considerably lighter now that half our food has been consumed.

"I had no idea how my body was going to hold up," Katie admits as the lake's foggy waters come into view. "But it feels amazing, for almost covering one hundred miles in four days."

"You can never really tell what might go right or wrong until you're out here." I pull myself up a large boulder with help from a balsam tree. "My doctor once told me not to do these things, either speed records or anything at high altitude, because they can cause flare-ups."

"I can see you aren't following that advice."

"No." I chuckle. "I told her that wasn't an option for me. And besides, in some ways the mountains level the playing field. Anyone can twist an ankle. Anyone can get GI distress. They make me feel more at home, because other hikers have to pay as much attention to their bodies as I do."

"That's a big reason I fell in love with this," Katie agrees. She crosses the small outlet of Feldspar Brook and sets her pack behind a large rock beside the herd path. "To be more mindful and intentional with my life."

Silently, we shift gears for the one-mile out-and-back to Gray, moving a water bottle and two rain shells to the daypack. The trail is all mud and rock. Shrubby branches scrape against our battered hands as we grasp them to haul ourselves to the top of our twentieth mountain just before noon. Katie snaps a photo of me looking at the summit sign with my hands pressed against my back. I dig my knuckles against my knotty muscles, which ache from four days of hiking, carrying a pack, sleeping on the ground, and menstrual cramps. At this point, it all melds together.

We hustle back to our packs and within an hour, we are on the open-domed summit of Mount Skylight. Now, most of the hiking is above 3,500 feet, so we won't lose as much elevation from peak to peak. It feels easy compared to the peaks and valleys of the Loj Loop. Katie and I sit for a moment to stretch. Grabbing my toes, I scan the overcast sky. It's almost 1 p.m. and there's still no rain and barely a breath of wind. *Maybe the weather forecast has changed? That would be amazing.* Even the temperature is pleasant, a refreshing day in the high fifties.

A ring of small stones encircles Skylight's summit marker. Katie and I push ourselves to a standing position and take a photo of our trail runners on either side of the rocks before heading back down.

.

Mount Marcy (5,344 ft.) — No. 22

WE DROP THE half mile from the summit of Skylight back to Four Corners, a well-marked intersection of four trails, before proceeding up Mount Marcy, the highest mountain in New York State. With the trekking poles, Katie takes point. Even at the modest pace she is setting, my calves scream against the steep rock slabs. I shift my gait to do a side step, searching for relief from the pressure.

On the backside of Marcy, a cold wind hits my body as we break the treeline. The barometric pressure is changing. Goose bumps rise on my arms. *That's okay. We're on an exposed summit that's usually windy.* Then it begins to sprinkle. *Okay, still okay. It's only a little rain.*

"I'm gonna get my rain jacket on," I yell above the wind.

"Me too!"

I quickly pull off my pack and dig around for my jacket. My fingers clench tightly around the slick fabric, so it doesn't blow away. The wind pushes at me as I struggle into the coat and zip it up to my neck before lacing my waterproof pack cover over the top and bottom of my pack.

Adorned in our rain gear, Katie and I continue up the angled rock slab. *Okay, still okay. Let's get up and over this mountain,* I tell myself. *We'll have more protection on the other side.* Then a gust of wind nearly knocks me to my knees. Leaning into it, I clap my hands over my nose to recover my breath. The wind whips around and rain intensifies, slickening the rock beneath our trail runners. *Just get to the top. It's close.*

With nowhere to go but up, Katie and I reach the 5,344-foot summit of Mount Marcy a little after 1:30 p.m. While Katie digs out her cell phone for the picture, I grasp my pack cover on either side of my body, so it doesn't fly away into the dark abyss of Panther Gorge.

"Alright, let's get down." I lead a quick descent away from Four Corners and the route we ascended, toward the junction between Mount Haystack and the Great Range, eager to get out of the wind and back under the cover of trees. My hands are cold and white, the feeling sucked out of them. Rain hits the side of my face and trickles down my neck. *Fuck, this isn't good.* My intuition prickles.

The High Peaks are no joke, and the Great Range, where we are spending the day, contains Mount Marcy and some of the tallest and fiercest mountains in the Northeast. Many fatalities in the Adirondacks occur in this area, under these conditions. It's naive and dangerous to underestimate the mountains of the East Coast because of their relatively small size compared to peaks out West. The terrain is rugged, the weather can change rapidly, and there is no one to readily come to your rescue.

With mountain ghosts and the hypothermic rainstorm at the forefront of my mind, I shiver. The pressure to get this right weighs heavily on me. Not all mountain enthusiasts look at speed hiking favorably and can be quite critical when a fast-packing adventure goes awry. Women especially are more likely to be blamed for putting themselves at risk because of their "inexperience" compared to men who attempt the same feats. "They didn't know what they were doing," people will say. "They didn't have the proper gear and shouldn't have even been out there in the first place." I know every decision we make as the storm progresses will be scrutinized through the lens of hindsight—something we unfortunately don't have access to at the moment.

We re-enter the treeline, escaping the direct impact of the falling rain. However, low shrubby trees brush against our bodies, depositing their collected moisture. Within minutes, I'm completely soaked. The cold wind pushes me to move faster, my body going into survival mode.

Katie falls behind.

At the junction for Slant Rock Lean-to, I stop and stare at the sign. Water drips off my numb fingertips onto the earth. My lower half is completely saturated. I regret not bringing rain pants, but at this point, I'm not sure how much good they would do.

"Come on, Katie. Come on, Katie," I mutter to myself, glancing back up the trail while swinging my arms in circles to stay warm. My core temperature is dropping by the second. A few minutes pass, no Katie. A violent shiver wracks my body. The longer I don't move, the faster my mind spins.

Maybe we should drop to the lean-to for shelter; maybe we should keep going. The lean-to is a mile away with a loss of one thousand feet in elevation. If we go there and wait out the storm for the rest of the day, we'll fall behind the overall record pace by about twelve hours. But Snowbird, a high elevation campsite, is just half a mile up higher on the range. If we continue there and set up our tent, we'll still be exposed to the wind, but we won't lose as much ground. We could stay on pace if the storm passes quickly.

Below the treeline and without cell service, we have no way of knowing what the storm will or will not do. It's impossible to calculate the right decision. If we keep moving instead of taking shelter, our next mountain is Haystack, the third highest of the 46 High Peaks, which has a fully exposed summit. Even if we push on and complete the out-and-back to Haystack safely, we'll still have to continue along the Upper Range, which has few places to take shelter besides Snowbird because of the high elevation. At this pace and under these conditions, I don't think I'll be able to keep warm.

Factoring into each option is our responsibility to stay safe while attempting this FKT. It's not only the judgement of others that will befall us if things go wrong. Katie and I have chosen to push ourselves in the mountains during a global pandemic with minimal food and gear, when backcountry resources are already stretched thin and needed elsewhere. It's crucial that we make the right decision. To me, that fine line is part of the allure of an unsupported FKT. We've whittled our packs to the absolute essentials, hoping they will be enough. If it turns out that we've miscalculated, we must bow out.

Standing at the junction, I realize my jacket is no longer waterproof as frigid rainwater seeps against my skin. Bitterly, I ball my bloodless fingers into fists. Katie is nowhere to be seen. *Maybe I should backtrack and find her? What if she twisted an ankle and fell? I'll wait two more minutes. I'm sure she's coming.*

My animal body shivers and yearns to seek shelter, but my ego doesn't want to let go of the overall record. Four years ago, it was in this very spot between Mounts Marcy and Haystack that I made the gut-wrenching decision to end my second FKT attempt. But instead of being bitterly cold, my insides were baking in the heat. The prospect of history repeating itself, but on opposite ends of the temperature spectrum, feels too cruel. Too hot, too cold. My fists tighten. How many times will I get so close only to be so far away? How many times should I try to make something work? I keep thinking this time will be different. I have a strong partner.

I've learned so much in recent years. I put together the best ultralight kit possible. Just as I've spent the last few years trying anything and everything to make my marriage work. Another therapy session. Another gratitude practice. Another hike where I had to pry him out of the house. What difference can these things really make? Why do I keep coming back? I can't keep failing at everything. We have to finish.

Rationally, I know we can't continue to make record pace in these conditions, so we might as well try to wait it out. I also know there's no record worth putting our lives in jeopardy for. At this moment, Katie and I are both healthy and strong, but the storm is slowing us down and I'm struggling to stay warm. I feel my emotions cresting like waves. I fear I am approaching the gray area of making a poor decision in the backcountry.

Finally, Katie rounds the corner.

I shout above the wind, "I think we need to drop down to the lean-to."

"What?" She shouts back.

"I think we need to drop to Slant Rock," I repeat. "To wait out the storm."

"Really?" Katie asks. "What about Snowbird?" Her face is calm. Confused. Unlike me, she hasn't spent the last ten minutes spiraling into fear and agonizing over the right thing to do. She's been hiking, keeping a steady pace, and conserving her energy on the downhill.

"I don't know." I shiver, losing my ability to think clearly.

While waiting at the junction, a part of me has decided to go down, not up. But I don't want to dismiss Katie's opinion. She's my partner. My teammate. This is her record too. And I don't want her to feel like her pace is part of the equation. Even though it is. It has to be.

"I'll run ahead and see about Snowbird," I say, conceding that we can at least see if it's a viable option.

"Okay, I'll be right behind you," Katie says.

She follows me into the storm.

Snowbird Campsite (4,060 ft.)

ALONE ON TRAIL again, fear gnaws at my confidence as I slog through ankle-deep water. I try to push it aside, hoping Snowbird will be okay. But those fears are only confirmed when I arrive ten minutes later. Every campsite is a swimming pool. There is no place to set up a shelter. Wind howls through the trees.

"Fuck!" I yell at the rain. "And fuck you!" I yell at Daniel, even though he's miles away. I can't believe this is what my life has become. I'm a fucking failure. I'm failing at this, just like I'm failing at marriage. All I've done is hide his illness from the world. I've been saying I'm fine over and over again, but I'm not fine. I haven't been fine in a long time. I've been neglecting my health and sanity to keep pushing through. And this campsite isn't fine either. And we can't keep pushing through; we need to go down.

The call came a little over a year ago, from Daniel's childhood friend, as an April rainstorm passed through the valley.

"Daniel's an alcoholic," he told me.

"What?" The wind shifted and rain fell against the living room window, which stood ajar.

"Bethany, he's an alcoholic," he said more slowly. "He's with me now and I'm taking him to an AA meeting tonight. He's had a problem for years."

Tears came faster than words. Love for Daniel was replaced by sadness.

Long after the conversation ended, I sat on the couch with Tahawus's warm body nestled against my legs. Numb. Rain had fallen through the open window, and I stared at the puddles on the living room floor. Puddles of tears. There was no denial, no anger. Not even irritation that he had confided in a friend and not me, his wife. I was grateful he had finally told someone, something that our society does not readily allow boys and men to do. I had known for so long that something had wrapped itself around his neck. Now I had a name for it. Alcoholism.

"It all makes sense," I whispered, my body shivering. Pieces of the puzzle I could never quite figure out started falling into place. The growing distance. The mistrust. The lies.

"Yes, I paid that bill," he'd say.

"No, you didn't. I got a call that it's past due."

"But I did. It must be a mistake. I'll look into it."

The first time it happened, I believed Daniel. It must've been a mistake. He was such a dependable person. The second time, I still believed him.

But now, it was easy to see he had been hiding behind forgetfulness and mistakes. Each word and story was crafted to hide his addiction from me. It wasn't a new deodorant. It was alcohol.

There had been clues besides the unpaid bills and fruity scent radiating from his skin.

The meals that went uneaten.

"Daniel, you haven't eaten anything all day."

"I had a big sandwich for lunch."

"Oh yeah? From where?" I had begun playing detective, like a suspicious mother. But I didn't know what I was looking for.

The tubes of toothpaste and mouthwash.

"Why do you have a toothbrush in your backpack?"

"Oh, I like to brush my teeth at work after lunch."

The tobacco.

"Are you chewing tobacco?" I'd ask.

"Oh no, I was out playing disc golf with the guys and they had some."

Finally, I didn't feel like I was losing my mind anymore. But this felt worse. Much worse. Sickeningly worse. It was like I'd been living in a black-and-white fog, then those three words—"Daniel's an alcoholic"—flipped my vision to color.

Suddenly all I could see were hiding spots. I ripped up the couch cushions and found a stash of chewing tobacco.

I went to the kitchen and pulled a heavy-duty garbage bag from the storage cabinet. I threw the tobacco into it, hearing the metal can clink against the kitchen floor through the bag.

With shaking hands, I tore the house apart, as easily as those lies had torn up my mind. I opened drawers, pushed up ceiling tiles, sifted through the pile of clothes he kept on his closet floor. After only an hour of searching, I had filled two black garbage bags with alcohol and tobacco. I lugged them to the front porch and set them out in the rain. I wanted every last bottle and chew can out of my house. I wanted every piece of evidence—of his betrayal, of my blindness—out. I wanted him out. I even wanted myself out of this house.

My legs buckled beneath me. *Who was Daniel? How could he have done this to us?* During our time in wilderness therapy, we had promised to share everything with each other. We saw what could happen to a family with secrets. A family who didn't know how to talk about hard things. *Hadn't I been supportive and kind? Didn't he know he was safe to tell me anything? I wasn't only his wife, I was his best friend.* Early in our relationship and wilderness therapy days, we talked passionately about the difference in cultural expectations of men and women, when it came to asking for help. We agreed that the stigma around men's vulnerability was stupid—that teaching men to suppress emotions was harmful. We pledged that if we had a son, we wouldn't raise him any differently than a daughter when it came to talking about their feelings.

We'd had conversations about how he didn't want to end up like people in his family who struggled with addiction. He was always the designated driver when we went out to dinner, so I could have a drink or two with my burger and sweet potato fries. We didn't even keep alcohol in the house, except for the occasional bottle of wine. Or so I thought.

Suddenly, I questioned every detail about our life together. Nausea came over me. I gasped for breath. I didn't even know who I was married to. If I left now, I wouldn't be seen as the fiercely independent woman who chose the mountains over marriage. I'd be seen as the woman who abandoned her alcoholic husband when he needed her the most. I'd be a traitor to what I believed in. Abandoning my professional training when it hit too close to home. There was no winning. No happy ending. After minutes sobbing on the floor, I grabbed my wallet and got in my minivan with Tahawus. I didn't know where I was going, but I needed to leave.

Three hours later, I pulled into my parent's driveway. I fled to the only home that felt safe to me now.

"It's flooded," I report when I reach Katie back on the trail. I'm colder and wetter than I'd been at the Slant Rock Junction. My maxi pad slips to the side of my underwear, and I cup it back into place. Trying to compose myself after my little freak-out moment, the anxious adrenaline continues to pump through me, clouding my brain.

"What if we tried to set up here?" Katie points to a shrubby patch of forest not too far from the main Snowbird site.

I don't say anything for a long moment. It's not ideal, but it's not horrible either.

"We should at least try," Katie insists.

I look up and down the trail, still unable to speak, trying to comprehend how quickly the record is slipping away from us, wondering if I'm in any state to make the call. Maybe Katie is right. She seems more clearheaded than I am. My head falls into my hands. *Focus, Bethany. Think!* The tent is safe and dry in my pack. If I pull it out here, everything will be exposed to the elements. I don't want to open my pack. *But maybe we should try. Maybe this will work. Maybe the storm is about to pass. Maybe I'll regret it if we don't try. Come on, Bethany, fight! Don't flee.*

Finally, I nod. "Okay."

We step off the trail and I unclip my pack to dig for the bundled tent inside. Katie grabs a corner and helps spread the fabric taught. Fighting against the wind, it takes us multiple attempts to secure the poles into the corners. Within minutes, I regret our decision. *This is crazy. What are we doing?* We aren't far from Slant Rock Lean-to, a perfectly secure structure where we could dry our gear and clothes. Even if we manage to set up the tent in the storm, all we'll be able to do is hunker down until the storm passes, which could take the rest of the day. We won't be able to dry anything. Our clothes and bodies will still be wet, cold messes. The logical half of my brain roars to life and scolds my hands for even taking the tent out of my pack.

By the time we get the tent set up, the remainder of my gear, which had been somewhat protected inside my pack, is now wet. Now all we have for our efforts is an unstable shelter and more gear in need of drying. Nonetheless, I remove my shoes and crawl in.

Water gushes through the tent floor everywhere my weight rests. I violently shiver as I rip off my socks, pants, jacket, synthetic top, and sports bra as quickly as I can. In only a pair of bikini briefs, I rummage through my pack for something dry, but there's nothing. My sleeping bag is damp and even my maxi pad is waterlogged. Water continues to seep in through the bottom of our tent.

"This is so fucking stupid," I mumble to myself.

Nearly naked, I stare at my bruised thighs and calves. *This isn't working.* No matter how much I want it to. No matter how much I need it to. No matter how much I believe we can do it. In the past, if I was in a hard or dangerous situation in the mountains, I had been spurred on by an image of home. A heartfelt bear hug from Daniel, where I'd leap into his arms and wrap my legs around his waist, and we'd laugh about how my armpits smelled like onions. To warm blankets, a pizza in the oven, and a cuddle with my pup. Rain pelts the tent. That home isn't there anymore.

These mountains have become the closest thing I have to a safe place. My tent. My pack. Now this is where I run when things get hard. Even as they turn against me, I don't want to abandon them. I hate how I seem unable to let go. To surrender. I keep coming back to the white board and trying again. *Why can't I move on? Just give up? Wouldn't things be easier if I did?*

Katie stands shivering in the doorway of the tent. My palms grow clammy. There's no way we can stay safe in this shelter in these conditions.

"Fuck!" I scream like a feral woman, crouched in nothing but my underwear and soggy pad.

Katie's eyes go wide. Her bluish lips tremble.

"We have to go down. Now!"

It isn't a question or debate anymore. Katie looks away from my angry almost-nakedness and doesn't protest. I try to summon the energy to put my wet clothes back on and venture into the storm. Instead, I sit frozen and stare at my pale, veiny feet. My right foot still has a bump on the top from breaking it when I was ten years old at my grandparent's house. I remember the look on my mother's face when she came to take me to the hospital. The one that said, *I know you are in pain, but you are here because of a careless decision you made.* I wonder what she would think if she saw me here in the middle of the storm, cold and nearly naked in the middle of the Adirondack wilderness, feeling defeated and sorry for myself. Letting my emotions take over in a crisis. Having a meltdown.

Katie and I are here because of me and my decade-long dream. I'm the one who talked her into making a speed attempt and pushing the clock. She had only cared about completing the route at first, but then my ambition became hers too. I told her we could do this and I need to keep us safe. The situation is deteriorating fast, and we are on our way to hypothermia. I need to put on my clothes and get moving. I need to do this for Katie. My mom. My family. Me.

"Aaaaah!" I scream as I shimmy back into my cold, waterlogged pants. "Everything is fucking wet."

Katie reaches into her pack and generously passes me her dry fleece. I put it on and zip my rain jacket over it. Teeth rattling, I jam my pruney feet back into my shoes and emerge from the tent. My wet layers and gear are a sopping mound; I stuff it all into my pack. Not a word is uttered as Katie and I tear down the tent.

Get down, get down, get down. I pray for us to make it down the mountain safely. *Get down, get down, get down.* With everything packed up, I throw on my pack and hustle down the trail, sticking my fingers under my armpits. My shoelace catches on a root and I stumble forward, almost face-planting onto a large rock. My body jerks and I slow my pace. We need to get down in one piece.

At the junction for Slant Rock Lean-to, we veer away from the

Great Range, abandoning the mountains we still need to climb. Just like that, it's done and the world around me is suffocatingly gray. I don't care about the thru-hike anymore. Striving for impossible things is a stupid waste of time. How childish I was to think this could heal something in me. Or somehow save my marriage to Daniel. My lip quivers and I bite down on it. Tears won't change a damn thing. Like the cold, it's better not to feel.

Slant Rock Lean-to (3,368 ft.)

THE LEAN-TO SITS on top of a small hill, and I can't tell if it's occupied or not.

Please be empty, please be empty, I pray as I race uphill to the wooden structure. A few steps later, I crest the hill and find no signs of inhabitants.

"Oh, thank you, thank you." I tilt my head toward the stormy heavens.

On opposite sides of the lean-to, Katie and I buzz about like mad bees, emptying our packs and wringing out our clothes. With each twist, water runs over my hands and forms puddles at my feet. Within minutes, our tent, clothes, and gear occupy every beam and nail in the lean-to. I take off my soaking shoes and prop them against the wall. Water pools in the heels. Wind rips down the mountainside. Now that we are out of the rain, the long drying process begins.

For the first time in four days, my body feels clean, like I just stepped out of nature's shower. In the wetness of my hair, I can faintly smell the remnants of shampoo. My synthetic pants and Katie's borrowed fleece dry quickly in the wind, but my underwear is soaked. I strip down behind the lean-to.

"Ugh." I groan as the absorbent pad falls to the ground with no adhesion left. Looks like I'll be free bleeding for a bit until my underwear dries. I wring out the pad and stuff it in my garbage bag.

In the far corner of the lean-to, Katie and I set aside anything dry. It's not much, but gradually I transition out of survival mode and begin to relax. We have shelter. We have food. We are injury free. *Okay, we can make this work.* Even my body is beginning to warm, and color is returning to my fingertips.

I wish this lean-to had a fire pit, so Katie and I could build a fire. But in the central High Peaks, campfires are forbidden. During the 1970s, a significant uptick in hiking and camping in the Adirondacks led to an increase of campers cutting down live trees to feed their fires. And in some cases, even hacking off chunks of wood from lean-to shelters for easy fuel. The central High Peaks around Mount Marcy saw the worst of it. Because of the remote location, rangers found it hard to monitor appropriate fire use, so it was easiest to ban them all together. Only in a true survival situation can you resort to fire making. Katie and I may be cold and damp, but we'll certainly live now that we are out of the elements.

I twist my wet hair into a high bun. Katie sits against the back of the lean-to and stares out at the whipping wind and rain. The surrounding peaks are encased in a thick blanket of clouds.

"I'm sorry I yelled earlier," I say, shaking water from my ground pad and sitting next to her. "That really scared me. And I had this horrible feeling and all I could think about was getting us down. And I thought about my mom . . ."

"I know," Katie cries and her face falls into her hands. "I'm so sorry."

"It's okay." I sympathize. "It's okay. We're okay."

"No, no, we should have descended when I got to the junction," she says. "I didn't know how cold you were and didn't want to let go of the record."

"I know, I know," I say. "I didn't want to let go of it either. And I certainly couldn't think or even talk straight up there in the storm."

Together we absorb the truth. Here we are, in nothing but our base layers, sitting on the floor of the lean-to at 3 p.m., while the clock continues to tick.

"We're safe," I reassure Katie. To keep our minds occupied and determine what the next few days will look like, I suggest, "Let's do a food inventory and ration for an extra day."

Katie lifts her head, wiping her eyes with the back of her hand. Together we begin counting calories. I lay out my bags and remove a little food from each one, gradually filling my empty day one bag. "It will be tight, but we can do it."

"And we can share a dinner tonight since we're burning less calories," Katie suggests.

We spend the rest of the day rotating clothes, nibbling on food, talking about our childhoods and late introductions to hiking, and waiting for the rain to pass. It finally clears around 6 p.m. The sky remains ominous, and the wind continues to howl down from the Great Range. With damp gear and no place to shelter up high, we accept we won't be continuing our mission today.

"At least we'll get some time off our feet." I try to lighten our situation, even though I know I'd rather be moving than sitting in this shelter surrounded by damp gear.

"Maybe that will help us in the long run. I hope Kenny doesn't get too worried when he doesn't hear from me tonight." Katie shakes her head fondly, thinking of her husband. "He's such a worrier."

"Hopefully he'll assume no news is good news," I offer.

Darkness falls and we stash our bear canisters away from the lean-to. We gather our dry sleeping gear to one side of the hut so we can share Katie's tarp as a blanket for additional warmth. My sleeping bag is still too damp to use, so I crawl into my sleeping bag liner. With the tarp, it's actually quite cozy. We lie on our backs and talk about silly things like how painful it is to pee in the woods after one hundred miles. I'm reminded of teenage sleepovers I used to have at my girlfriends' houses. When we shift our positions, the tarp crinkles and we laugh at our ingenious setup. And like when I was young, somewhere in the middle of conversation I drift off to sleep.

Day Five

September 14, 2020
14.7 miles
7,800 feet vertical gain

Mount Haystack (4,960 ft.) — No. 23

A SOLID TEN hours of sleep later, I swing my legs out of the lean-to and look up toward the Great Range, which is still encased in a low bank of fog. Gone is the cocoon-like warmth of my sleeping bag liner, replaced by damp morning air hitting the back of my neck, causing a shiver to run the length of my body. Yesterday, the rain continued into the evening, and the sky never cleared. At least the wind partially dried our gear, taking it from sopping wet to merely damp.

"Ah, it's so cold." I recoil as my fingertips touch the moisture-laden fabric of my sports bra. Without another thought, I push the bra aside, knowing I'm going to hike without it until I'm fully warmed up.

Behind the lean-to, I step out of my pants and put on a pair of underwear that spent the night in the bottom of my sleeping bag liner and is mercifully dry. With stiff fingers, I open the yellow plastic packaging on my second-to-last maxi pad. It adheres perfectly to the fabric. I hitch up my underwear and the pad settles into place. While pantiless, I'd wadded up a piece of toilet paper to act as a makeshift pad last night. Thankfully, my period hasn't been too heavy and only a small amount of blood got on my black sleep pants.

"How'd you sleep?" I ask Katie when I come back to the lean-to.

"Good, all those hours felt luxurious."

Since Katie and I have already abandoned the overall record by dropping to the lean-to, we figured we might as well get a full night's sleep to reset our bodies and mission.

The extra weight of my damp gear and clothing drops onto my shoulder straps as we descend from the lean-to. It feels like day one all over again. As we make our way back to the trail, I carefully pick my way through the saturated forest, doing my best to avoid outstretched tree branches holding buckets of water in their leaves. The terrain ascends quickly and my body warms. It's time to change.

"I'm doing it. I'm stripping," I warn Katie.

"I'll give you some space." She laughs before continuing up the trail. This privacy is purely symbolic for at this point our bodies hold few secrets from each other. The rules of modesty dissipate the longer one is on trail.

To my left there is a large flat rock, and I place my pack on top of it. I dig out my damp hiking top and peel off Katie's fleece. For a moment, I press its warmth to my face before reaching for my soggy pink sports bra.

"Come on, Bethany," I say, trying to hype myself up like I do before jumping off a cliff into a cold lake. My arms shimmy through the wet bra. I shriek as it encases my chest. "Ah! Ah!"

Goose bumps erupt down my arms and my nipples harden before I can even pull on my green top and rain jacket.

"Ah, ah!" I keep hyperventilating as I clip into my pack and jog to catch up with Katie.

"All good?" she asks as I come charging up behind her.

"Yes," I say panting. "Yes."

Finally my body is warm. I tuck my fingers under my chest straps.

The tops of the trees above us sway back and forth. Hopefully the wind will blow the fog out. I return my gaze to following Katie's feet and barely notice the junction when she veers slightly left. But out of the corner of my eye, I catch a glimpse of the simple wooden sign where we stopped yesterday, caught in a debate between fear and ambition. It stands as a reminder of just how quickly a plan can change.

Back on the Great Range and nearly a day behind schedule, we retrace our steps toward the spur for Haystack.

"It's about half a mile from here," I say, dropping my pack to the side of the trail. Katie follows suit and we layer up, forgoing even the daypack for this short out-and-back. We climb up rock slabs and are quickly above the treeline. I pull on my hat and gloves in response to a fierce wind. Surrounded by dense fog, it's hard to believe one of the most stunning views of the 46 High Peaks can be found here. I try to picture it as the wind pummels the back of my head.

A few hundred feet from the summit of Haystack there is only fog. I feel empty and disconnected from our mission. *What does it matter anyway?* We've lost the record. Around 8:30 a.m., Katie and I tap our shoes against the summit marker.

"Number twenty-three," Katie announces. "Halfway to forty-six."

"Uh-huh." I try to bury my disappointment under my jacket's hood.

Without the storm, we'd be on our thirtieth summit this morning. Now when we finish, all people will see is that we were slower than the men. Just like everyone thought we would be. On top of that bitter thought, my pack is sitting on the damp ground still loaded with damp gear. And from what I can remember about the forecast, tonight will be the coldest yet—possibly in the twenties. How will we sleep if our gear hasn't fully dried? Maybe we'll have to keep moving to stay warm. But that will take more calories. We're already running on a spartan gear list, and now we'll have to eat a little less each day to make it to the end. If we resupply our food, our attempt is no longer unsupported. It's bad enough we won't beat the men's time, but if we can't finish unsupported, I don't want to finish at all. As Katie and I scamper down from the summit, I look to the east.

Where is the sun? We need the sun.

Basin Mountain (4,827 ft.) — No. 24
Saddleback Mountain (4,515 ft.) — No. 25

As we hike past the Snowbird campsite, I clamp my lips together and keep my head down, focusing on my feet and the trail beneath them. *Breathe, breathe. Fuck the storm. Breathe, breathe. Fuck you, Snowbird.* The Basin Mountain cliffs are slick, so Katie and I slow our pace to navigate the dangerous terrain, where one misstep could result in a concussion or broken leg. Even though I'm questioning everything through a hypercritical lens, I know we made the right decision to drop down to Slant Rock during the storm. The rugged exposure of Haystack and Basin remind me that if something had gone wrong in this section, the consequences could have been dire.

The summit of Basin Mountain is another rocky, treeless landscape blanketed in fog. We take a quick picture and walk over the summit. The Great Range is a sequence of eight High Peaks, beginning with Mount Marcy and ending with Lower Wolf Jaw. Our original plan was to complete the entire range yesterday. Yet here we are. I trudge onward in a funky, foggy purgatory, wondering if Katie shares my feelings of defeat and surrender.

"Maybe we should call it?" I finally pose aloud in the col

between Basin and Saddleback Mountains.

"Call what?" Katie asks.

"The thru-hike. Maybe say this was a practice run and come back next year? We could continue to train over the winter and spring."

I'm actually a little excited at the prospect of having something to do for the foreseeable future. And the idea of building on this budding friendship and trail partnership.

Katie pauses on the ledge she's navigating and looks back at me. For a moment, I think she's going to agree with me, but then she shakes her head. "I'm going to finish. A woman needs to finish this."

"But we can't beat the overall record," I say. "And I'm so tired of women coming in second to men. We can get the overall if we come back next year."

"I know, but I really don't care if it's the overall record or the women's record. It matters that a woman does this." Katie protests. "I don't even care if it's unsupported or if I run out of food and need to get a resupply—I'm finishing this hike."

"But it *does* matter to me if it's unsupported. And the fastest. It always has."

Katie and I look away from each other. My eyes focus on the far-off triangular summit of Whiteface Mountain. Every journal, every sketch, every Excel spreadsheet flashes before my eyes. I think about all the times I mapped out this route. I knew the math, the pace, the terrain, and what my body could do. Not simply to make a point that women are fast and strong and can do this. But because I felt called to complete it.

And maybe it doesn't have to be about beating the men. Maybe it never was. Do women have to beat men to prove we are worthy? Or that we belong? Isn't being out here enough? Instead of dropping to try again, what if we kept going and let it be what it was? Second place still gets a medal.

The day I found out Daniel was an alcoholic, I cried for 150 miles and showed up on the front porch of my childhood home with swollen eyes. My parents and I sat around the kitchen table and talked for hours—going over the years one by one and noting in hindsight a general decline in his health and sense of self.

"I was so worried the last time I saw him," my mother said sympathetically—finally acknowledging what I'd been trying to figure out for years. "I'm so sorry."

"At least now we know what's going on." I felt a twinge of something I hadn't felt in a long time. Hope. If we knew what was wrong, we could fix it.

That evening as the rain finally cleared, I walked the tractor lane out to the backwoods on my parents' property, where Daniel and I had begun building a rustic cabin two years earlier. I had sensed he was struggling, so I created a project for us to work on together. Whenever we came out to the cabin, he lit up like his old self—I could see him finding purpose, if only for a few hours.

Standing in those backwoods, surrounded by salvaged beams dating from the 1800s, I watched a hawk circle above me. Daniel and I had a solid foundation to work from. We could do this. I'd get some rest and return to him in the morning. I'd help him get the treatment he needed. Whatever it cost. He could be sober. Our marriage might not look the way I'd always imagined. There would be blemishes and scars. But we could keep building on this beautiful thing we'd started.

A warm wind touches the back of my neck, causing me to shiver. It's time. It's time to move forward, to embrace a different objective. It won't look like I thought it would, and maybe that's a good thing. I'm not the same barefoot girl who began hiking in the High Peaks. I'm not the idealistic young woman who married Daniel on a dock with flowers in her hair. I've become someone else, and I'm meeting her out here.

"Okay," I stammer. "I'll keep going."

"Good." Katie turns away, not giving my doubt another thought.

As we navigate the steep cliffs of Saddleback Mountain, I'm embarrassed about my lapse in motivation. I think about the blessing I felt on Allen, when the sun set a brilliant orange and pricked the hairs on my arms. We are meant to finish what we started.

"Thanks for pulling me through that," I say.

"Anytime," she says more softly. "We got this."

I nod and glance up at the sky. "Now we just need the sun to come out. Some of my gear is still pretty wet."

"It will," Katie assures me.

She's so sure. I have to believe she is right.

We climb the cliffs hand over hand, picking our lines through the cracks and spotting each other in the trickiest sections. Brown grasses sprout from the patches of soil that cling to flatter sections of rock. I wedge my foot in a crack and pull myself upward; the coarse surface scrapes the palms of my hands. Following the yellow blazes, we arrive on the summit and look back toward Basin. Patches of blue speckle the sky to the north. Light touches my shoulder.

Here comes the sun. Here comes my future.

Sawteeth (4,100 ft.) — No. 26
Gothics (4,736 ft.) — No. 27

"Come on, sun! Come on, sun! Sun, sun, sun!" I cheer, thrusting my trekking poles wildly at the sky.

"Come on!" Katie joins in and pauses to stretch her calves on the notoriously steep incline toward our next two High Peaks, Gothics and Sawteeth. We've gained five hundred feet in less than a quarter mile.

I bring the trekking poles down and lean into them for a full hamstring stretch. "Ahhh, that feels amazing."

Gothics was named for its sheer cliffs, especially on the north side, and arched peak resembling a middle ages cathedral. Cable lines run along the ledges for hikers to steady themselves as they ascend and descend near the precipitous drop-offs. We are ascending toward Gothics but will take a quick detour to Sawteeth before reaching the summit.

I grasp the rusty cables with my hands to pull my way up the steep rock face. My calves burn and my heart thuds against my rib cage. I pause again to stretch. The thick layer of fog we've been living in finally begins to lift, allowing beams of sunlight to fall around us. Steam rises from the slick rock, burning off the remnants of yesterday's storm.

"Let's dry out our stuff when we get to the turnoff for Sawteeth," I suggest.

With the summit of Gothics in sight, Katie and I veer right onto a trail that will take us over Pyramid Peak to Sawteeth, our twenty-sixth High Peak.

Off the main trail but still on open rock, Katie and I find a place to open our packs and put together our daypack for the difficult out-and-back to Sawteeth. A mile and a half to the summit, with a 900-foot drop down to the saddle followed by a 600-foot climb, the idea of completing it and then immediately reversing back to our packs makes me queasy.

"Ah, Sawteeth," I grumble to myself.

Katie and I will be gone for a couple of hours, so I place heavy rocks on top of my sleeping bag to keep it from blowing away. Then I clip the damp pack with my remaining gear to another rock. It's a gamble, but at this point, we have to gamble a bit. We will only have a certain amount of time above the treeline, and right now the sun is shining. The promise of a completely dry sleeping bag is worth the small risk it may wander off while we are gone. Plus, it's more efficient to leave it here in the sun unattended than for us to stop and waste time sunning our gear.

If it were the peak of summer and we had night temperatures in the high sixties, I wouldn't be so anxious. But as fall approaches, temperatures drop below freezing at night, so I don't want an ounce of moisture in my gear once the sun goes down. To keep our bodies functioning, we need to sleep. And to sleep well, we need warm, dry gear.

From back on the trail, I look over my shoulder to make sure our gear is hidden from sight. Through all my years hiking, I've only had a few issues with other hikers happening upon stashed items. Once, I made the mistake of hanging a brand-new fleece on a tree branch right next to the trail only to find it missing when I came back through. Hopefully if any hikers spot our gear today, it will be obvious we intend to return for it.

Katie leads the descent. I take off my quick-dry long-sleeve top, so my arms and shoulders can absorb the sun's piercing rays through the late morning crispness. Clear blue skies surround us as we dip down to Pyramid Peak, and I put in my earbuds. To my right, I can see the rocky backsides of Basin, Haystack, and Marcy, a jagged reminder of what we have endured to get here.

During detox, Daniel looked like he had the flu. On the day I returned from the cabin, we dedicated ourselves to cleaning the house and washing the piles of clothes that had accumulated in his closet. I drove the two garbage bags of nicotine and bottles, which had gotten soaked in the rain, to the dump while his friend took him to another meeting.

The next day, we went to a yoga class. His pale, sweaty body gave off the fruity scent of a mixed drink as the alcohol burned out of him. Unable to do any balance poses without shaking, he lay on his back in corpse pose for most of the class, returning from the land of the dead.

A few days later, I took him on a beginner-level rock climb, hoping that a new sport would ignite something in him. I tightened the rope and called out, "On belay!" He barely made it six feet off the ground before his trembling fingers lost their grip on the holds.

"This is so hard," he sighed, though appreciative of my efforts to bring him back to the world of being physically active. "I'm so sorry."

He went to meetings every day. After two weeks of sobriety, the color returned to his face. It was like running into a friend I hadn't seen since college, knowing how they once looked but having forgotten over the years. But with the clarity of a sober mind came glaring shame.

"I can't believe I put you through that for years," he'd often say.

"It's a disease," I'd respond. Though I felt utterly betrayed he had kept it a secret from me. I would have said more, but I feared the truth of what I had endured would break him. He had never wanted to hurt me. He had never wanted to become what he had grown up with. So I kept it to myself, while he did everything he could to keep his mind busy.

In the following months rock climbing replaced drinking. Daniel pushed his body obsessively. If he wasn't progressing, he felt like he was failing. It didn't take long before it stopped being fun to climb with him. By midsummer, I hung up my harness. When his climbing stalled around 5.10s and 5.11s—respectable mid-level climbs, especially for a beginner—he turned to running. Soon he bought a pair of barely-there shorts and a GPS watch.

"Can you drop me off at March Field?" he asked me one sweltering ninety-degree day.

"Are you sure?"

"Uh-huh, I want a good sweat."

Reluctantly, I pulled my minivan into the parking area and he bolted out, without even stretching. I watched as he pushed the start button on his watch and chased those five-minute miles. He was using the things we used to love to do together to punish himself. Every day.

He was sober now, but this was a whole new kind of pain to watch.

By the time Katie and I return to our gear after completing the three-mile out-and-back to Sawteeth, all the items we set out in the sun are dry. I hold the swishy fabric of my sleeping bag up to my face and exhale. "Hallelujah."

"We got everything?" Katie asks.

We swivel our heads around, triple checking every piece of precious gear has been packed away.

"I believe so." I scan the trees while clipping into my pack. "Oh! This feels so much lighter!" I bounce up and down.

The summit of Gothics is only a few minutes away. The northern side of the mountain cuts away to the Johns Brook Valley. From the edge of the monolith, I peer down. Fall color brightens the valley floor, mostly maple trees that are beginning to turn red and orange. On the other side of the river, another ridge of mountains rises. The most distinctive peak is Big Slide, with its sheer 1,000-foot rock face. When viewed from a certain angle, it looks like a miniature version of Yosemite's El Capitan. Clouds rest above the Upper Range, splattering the mountains with patches of light and darkness. Blue skies still cover the lower range as Katie and I walk over the summit of Gothics and make our way toward Armstrong Mountain, another mile beyond.

There are a few groups of hikers on the trail with us today. All men. Listening to my music, I nod when they wave or smile. There's a disproportionate ratio of men to women in outdoor spaces. I know this, and I teach it in my classes. Menstruation cycles, organized religion, and gender roles all play a part in the unequal representation. It continues to baffle me that people who grow and bear children are cast as "weaker" when it comes to outdoor pursuits.

Thankfully, my family never subscribed to this logic. I was *expected* to be outside. I grew up in the countryside with my sisters and cousins. We explored the fields and woods around our house from a young age. My mother and grandmother shooed us out of the house so they could get their work done without us underfoot. We were in the gardens picking vegetables, in the barns feeding the calves, or along the creekside making forts. As I got older, I explored farther away from the houses and barns. Choppy faces of limestone called to me. I climbed their unstable routes, breaking off large chunks of rock in my hands and letting them roll down the hillside beneath me. Many times, I fell from those rocks—probably should have broken a bone or two—but somehow the earth caught me and I walked away, a little stunned and full of adrenaline. I never questioned that the woods and mountains were my place.

But Katie had been told the opposite.

"I don't want you out there," her father had repeated on more than one occasion. "It's too dangerous."

Katie had told me this on our first hike together. "He took my brother out, but not me. Simply because I was a girl."

"That's crazy," I said, angry that young girls, even in the United States, endured such chauvinistic attitudes from their own parents. It's easy for me to think we're culturally beyond this because I didn't experience such backward thinking in my youth. I like to believe we are constantly growing toward more acceptance and tolerance. Moments like this remind me that my experience isn't everyone's experience; the barriers we face aren't always the same.

I'm proud of Katie for standing up to me on that mountain. For saying she'd finish the thru-hike with or without me. I had been thinking I was out here to mentor and encourage her. That she needed me to help her believe she could do it. She knew better. This was her place and her goal too. And she was willing to do it on her own if needed.

If we had quit, it would only reinforce the idea that women weren't strong enough to become 46ers. *Oh, they got hit by a storm and got wet and quit. Boo-hoo, how soft. How fragile.* I hadn't been able to see that through my competitive fog. But Katie saw it differently. Maybe it's because of her father's words—doubt or disapproval can be powerful motivators. She isn't trying to prove she can do it better than men, but that she can do it. Period.

As I follow Katie to the summit of Gothics, I watch her arms flex as she grips rocky handholds to pull herself upward. Whitney

Houston blasts in my ears. *This is our time. This is our place. Thank God Katie didn't let me quit.*

Armstrong Mountain (4,400 ft.) — No. 28
Upper Wolf Jaw Mountain (4,185 ft.) — No. 29
Lower Wolf Jaw Mountain (4,175' ft.) — No. 30

THIS LOWER RANGE is not as steep as the cliffs of Basin or Saddleback, so we easily reach the summit of Armstrong Mountain in just thirty minutes.

"Wow, the range goes fast," Katie muses, looking back to Gothics.

"It's like a roller coaster of peaks." I eye the cloud mass that continues to creep our way before adding, "Let's take a long break on Upper Wolf Jaw and dry the rest of our stuff. It's the last good access to sunlight we'll have."

After another half-mile descent followed by a half-mile ascent, we arrive on the shrubby summit of Upper Wolf Jaw, whose name reflects its distinct shape. From a distance, the jagged ridgelines of Upper and Lower Wolf Jaw look like the sharp teeth of a wolf. We find an open area among the wolf's teeth to rest and spread out our remaining gear, mostly the delicate garments I didn't feel comfortable yard-saleing on the shoulder of Gothics. As we steadily lose elevation down the range, the terrain will become more crowded with trees. There will be little access to exposed rocks and sunlight the rest of the day.

"What time is it?" I ask Katie, stepping onto the bare summit rock and dumping my pack.

"About three," she says, looking at the GPS watch.

We're making good time. Even if we stay here for an hour, we could still reach the summit of Colvin and Blake after dark and be at our campsite at the base of Nippletop by 10 or 11 p.m.

I unlace my trail runners to release my feet for the first time today and send out a message to the group chat, *Drying gear on Upper Wolf Jaw, still in it. Hit with a storm yesterday and fell behind, but we're feeling good.* Without motion, my body begins to cool. I layer up with my polypro top and rain jacket. My sleeping bag and fleece liner drape limply over shrubby pines. Our tent is woven through the branches of another tree. Our damp garments are like odd ornaments hanging from every tree and bush around the summit rock.

"Oh shit," I gasp.

"What?"

"I have holes." I show Katie the two-inch gash in the bottom of my pack.

"Whoa, when did that happen?" she asks.

"Not sure," I say, looking around to see what might have caused it. My eyes come to rest on the aluminum bear canister. Though made from ultralight material, it has a sharp, circular edge to it. On descents over the Great Range, I have been lowering myself to a sort of crab walk, using my arms to save my calves and thighs from taking the brunt of the steep downhill. I'd apparently been scraping the bottom of my pack against the rocks too.

"Shit, this is pretty big," I say, staring at the cut.

"I have some patches in my pack," Katie offers, pulling out her first aid kit. "You never know what you might need out here."

She grabs my pack to size up a pre-cut patch for the hole. She meticulously places the patch, deftly smoothing it down and securing it with silver duct tape. "There you go, good as new."

"Beautiful!" I say.

While we sit and rotate our gear, we also cook our dinner. The stove purrs to life. We decide to split a Thanksgiving dinner to save food. The day hasn't been too exhausting, so hopefully we can afford the calorie cut.

Looking south, I take in the steep slides of Dix Mountain glaring in the sunlight while my bare feet dangle off the rock lip. Tomorrow Katie and I will be ascending that steep vertical mile to the summit. Thinking of the Dix range, I feel for the scab on my forehead from our rehearsal FKT. Half of it has flaked away in the last few days.

Katie looks at my well-bandaged foot. "How's your blister doing?"

"Oh, it's good. I just keep putting more tape over it."

"Ignorance is bliss."

"In this case, yes." I run my hands over the swishy fabric of the tent and sleeping bag liner. "Looks like everything is dry."

We begin grabbing gear off tree limbs and neatly placing everything back into our packs, like we're carefully packing Christmas ornaments away on the first of January.

This time, I stuff my sleeping bag in the bottom of my pack and gently place the bear canister on top, so its sharp edges don't contact Katie's fresh patch. Then I place all my other belongings around the sides of the bear canister to secure it.

"Alright, let's rock and roll," I say, flipping my sunglasses down from the crown of my head. Our packs are even lighter now that every single piece of our gear is dry, and we make our way from Upper Wolf Jaw to Lower Wolf Jaw with ease.

The afternoon light changes quickly as we drop from the Great

Range. Golden rays stream through the canopy as we hike among birch and maple forest to the East River Trail. Large cedars thread their roots along the stones of the riverbanks, and small waterfalls cascade to our left. The sweet smell of wet pine is released from the sun's waning warmth.

The East River Trail isn't a heavy use area, so the soil is less compacted than some of the more popular trails in the Great Range. Pine needles cushion the soles of our tired feet. From behind, I notice a slight limp to Katie's gait.

"How do you feel about doing Blake and Colvin tonight?" I ask, curious about this physical development.

While we were pinned in the lean-to by the storm, we had adjusted our itinerary, adding Blake Peak and Mount Colvin to our list of summits to finish today. That way we wouldn't be a whole day behind.

"My quads are a little tight, but I don't want to fall behind on our new plan."

"It's okay," I say honestly with no mixed feelings, wanting Katie to make the choice that's best for her body.

Since the overall record isn't the objective anymore, we might as well be cautious and get another solid night of sleep. I have covered mileage like this before, but this is the biggest effort Katie has ever done. I don't want her to push past the breaking point. I want us to finish strong.

"How about we rest up tonight and get an early start tomorrow?" I suggest.

"Sure, that works." Katie's hobble is more pronounced than I'd realized. "I'm sorry about this," she says. "I really don't know where it's coming from."

"Don't be sorry. We're still in this because of you."

In the waning daylight, Katie and I arrive at Gill Brook campsite, which is occupied by one other camper. A young man in a puffy yellow jacket rummages around the opening of his one-person tent while Katie and I claim an empty site on the other side. A large birch tree with golden leaves stands guard over our new home, its branches sheltering us from the descending cold of night.

"Ah!" I scream, dancing over to a circle of stones with charred sticks in the middle of it. "We can make a fire! How did I forget we could have fires here?"

"I guess I did too. Because it's AMR land, I assumed we couldn't."

The Adirondack Mountain Reserve, or AMR, is a slice of private land that cuts through the Ausable River Valley. Owned by the Ausable Club, this private land comes with additional rules, like no dogs on the property. There is even speculation that a permit system may be put in place to reduce the number of hikers who can access the area.

"I'm going to get some birch and hemlock." I stoop to grab a smooth piece of white birch bark off the ground. While I gather items for the fire, Katie takes our water bottles to the stream. In the firepit, I build a nest of kindling interwoven with birch bark. When I tear the papery white bark into thin strips, other colors like pink and yellow emerge in the shreds. These fibers hold the power of fire.

One piece of white bark shrivels into flame when I flick the lighter. I place it in the center of the dry kindling. I lay a handful of hemlock twigs and more strips of birch bark on top. Katie returns from the stream and passes me my water bottle.

"I already dropped it with iodine," she says.

"Thanks."

"Nice fire." She sits on a log and breathes deeply, content to be off her feet. "Oh shoot, I forgot to fill my other water bottle."

"Do you want me to go fill it?" I offer.

"No, it's okay. I should have enough to drink and then I'll fill it in the morning," she says. "I'm going to change in the tent."

"Okay," I say, adding more sticks to the fire.

As Katie hobbles away to change, the young man in the yellow puffy emerges from his tent and waves. Zipping up his jacket, he walks over to the fire pit.

"Howdy, neighbor," he says.

"Well, howdy."

"It's so nice to see a fire out here," he adds. "I'm Jake."

"Bethany. Thanks, just don't put any sticks on it," I instruct him.

Underneath a knit cap, Jake's brow furrows and he tilts his head to the side. "What do you mean by that?"

"Uh, my hiking partner and I are doing this big hike, and we can't receive any sort of aid from outside sources," I explain. "So we have to collect all the wood for this fire."

"Sure . . . but what kind of big hike?"

"Katie and I . . ." I nod toward the tent. "Are in the process of hiking all 46 High Peaks unsupported. You know, no crew, no car rides, no food drops."

"What?" Jake leans forward. "Holy shit, you're the two women I've been hearing about on Facebook!"

As if on cue, Katie emerges from the tent and joins us at the fire.

"Probably." I laugh. "Katie and I have been pretty out of touch with the world."

"That is so dope." He smiles. "What you're doing is insane."

I add more sticks to the growing fire. A smile creeps across my face.

"What are you hiking tomorrow?" he asks.

"Colvin, Blake, Nippletop, and Dial, then we'll bushwhack to the Dix Range," Katie says.

"So, you'll be doing nine High Peaks in one day?" He shakes his head. "Absolutely badass. I'm only doing Colvin and Blake."

"Well, that's badass too," I say with sincerity. One summit or two out here is still a worthy challenge, and we all come to the mountains for different reasons.

"Sure." He laughs.

"No really, it's a big deal to be out here." I look at him across the fire.

This is the first conversation I've had with someone besides Katie for five days and it's humbling, like a mirror held up to what we're really doing out here. The reflection is pure wonderment. We're on our way to complete what fewer than ten people have ever done. I think in all the years of planning and failed attempts, it was easy for me to focus on the logistics of the thru-hike, and somewhere in that, I began to lose the heart of it. The why of it. The sheer magic of it.

The night sky darkens from blue to deep purple to an empty moonless black, and the temperature plunges. At this moment, my heart is content. I am just a person sitting by a campfire in the mountains. That's all I need to be. I munch on some chocolate and nuts before stowing my bear canister away from camp. The fire burns down and we all retire to our tents.

"Good luck," Jake says to Katie and me. "I can't wait to hear about you two finishing this thing."

"Thanks," we say in unison.

"We'll try to be quiet in the morning when we make our way out of here," I add.

"Oh, don't worry about it. Make as much noise as you need to."

Katie and I wiggle into our sleeping bags, and before we go to sleep, Katie pulls out her iPhone. I lean in next to her and we look over our photos from the day, a little ritual we started while holing up in Slant Rock Lean-to during the storm.

"Look at that one!" Katie laughs. "We look like rock stars."

On Lower Wolf Jaw, both wearing our Goodr sunglasses, we pose for our summit selfie with our hands on our hips and chins tilted upward.

"Well, we are," I say. "Look at what we've done."

We didn't let the humidity stop us on day one, I made it through day two with no sleep, Katie kept going on day three after deeply bruising her knee, we survived the Great Range storm on day four, and we decided to keep going on day five—even despite knowing we wouldn't finish in time to beat the men. We have been kissed by rain and sun, we have been tested under pressure, and through it all, we have taken care of each other.

We are badass.

Day Six

September 15, 2020
17.8 miles
9,100 feet vertical gain

Mount Colvin (4,057 ft.) — No. 31
Blake Peak (3,960 ft.) — No. 32

By the light of our headlamps, Katie and I dismantle our camp as quietly as we can so as not to disturb Jake sleeping next door. A thin film of frost coats the top of our tent, crunching as I open the rain fly. My body yearns to move quickly in the freezing air.

My legs feel taunt and springy as I search for our bear canisters in the trees.

"Wow, they are getting light," I whisper to Katie, clouds of breath swirling upward as I set them down by the fire pit. I pull out a hard Clif bar and stow it in my pants pocket to soften.

Katie leads us out of camp. A few minutes later, we stop to fill our water bottles where a stream crosses the trail. Green and brown rocks, round and polished from the passing water, shimmer in the glow of our headlamps. With a lighter base weight, I am conscious of the added pounds the full water bottle brings to my pack. As the trail steepens, Katie's pace slows dramatically ahead of me, and her feet shuffle over the rocks. I notice she is still moving with a limp, barely bending her right knee at all.

"You okay?" I ask.

"My quads are still tight," she says with concern. "I probably should've drunk more water last night. I was so tired. I passed out before I could."

"It's okay, our bodies are going to be a little stiff doing what we're doing." I try to downplay my concern, but Katie's limp is worrisome.

"How about you take point?" Katie suggests.

"Sure." I continue up the carefully laid staircase of rocks, letting her fall in behind. I wonder about the hours of labor that went into this path; it must have taken some trail crew weeks if not months to build. I understand where Katie is coming from. When I am struggling with an injury on trail, I prefer not to have an audience following right behind me. Maybe she needs her space to assess what's going on with her body.

Instinctively I fall into a guiding pace. "Slowly, slowly," I tell myself. But even at this gait, when I turn back to check on her, the round orb of her headlamp shines dimly in the distance.

Something is wrong.

It's okay. I lie to myself. *She just needs time to warm up, and we'll be dropping our packs soon.*

By the time I reach the junction for Mount Colvin and Blake Peak, the sky is brightening. A few minutes later, Katie hobbles up, her demeanor stoic.

"Let's get some food and take a little break," I suggest.

"But we're falling off pace."

"A little, but we'll finish the day when we finish the day," I assure her. "And if your muscles are tight, your body needs more electrolytes and nutrients."

Katie nods. We sit on our packs to eat some breakfast, our supply shrinking with every meal. We're scheduled to run out of food in two days. If we hold this pace, we may not make it to the finish line unsupported.

Don't think about that. One mountain at a time, I remind myself as I load the daypack with food and water. Hopefully, it's only a muscle cramp that will work itself out. But I fear Katie is in more pain than she's letting on. *Maybe she tore or tweaked something on the descent from Lower Wolf Jaw? Maybe she's hitting her physical limit?*

"Here, you take these from here on out." I pass Katie the trekking poles. No matter what's happening with her legs, reducing the impact of these miles on her biggest muscles can only help.

"Okay," she agrees. "But let me know if you need them."

"I will." I nod. I know how hard it is for Katie to ask for help—I'm the same way, and so are many women in outdoor fields. Always wanting to appear strong, like nothing is wrong. When really true strength is seeking help when you need it.

The summit of Mount Colvin overlooks the spiny ridgeline of the Great Range. For a few minutes, Katie and I sit next to the summit marker stretching our calves. The bitter coldness of the night is burned off by the rising sun, and I adjust my layers for the descent.

"You know, my legs feel much better on the downhill." Katie maneuvers the steep slabs off the summit, anchoring herself to exposed tree roots.

"That's great," I say, hopeful whatever is going on with Katie's leg is working itself out.

Blake Peak lies over a mile away from Colvin with a brutally sharp descent and ascent between them—which we'll have to retrace to get back to the junction with our packs. When learning the names and routes of the High Peaks, I always remember Blake comes after Colvin because it is the *brutal* part. In the col between the two peaks, I pause to ask Katie, "Do you want to set the pace on the uphill?"

"No, keep going," she says. "I'll meet you on the summit."

The half mile to the summit is layered with steep rock slabs. A few hundred yards from the top, I wait on an outcrop for Katie so we can arrive together. Birds chirp in the canopy and flit from branch to branch. I can hear trekking poles ticking against the granite before Katie rounds the bend. Her eyes are cast downward, focusing on her next step. Behind her, a blurry orange trail runner speeds up the trail, then abruptly stops, staring at us.

"Oh my gosh! It's the 46er ladies!" He bobs up and down, his long, curly Jesus-like hair bouncing around his grinning face. "Oh my gosh, oh my gosh! Can I take a picture?" He claps his hands together.

"Sure." Katie and I exchange surprised glances and lean together while he digs an iPhone out of his running vest.

"I'm Jason," he says, placing his hand on his chest. "And I'm like your biggest fan. I'm out hiking for 46Climbs too!" He points to the 46Climbs logo on his T-shirt, snaps a few photos, and narrates a video. "Hey all, guess who I found on trail? The 46er ladies, Katie and Bethany!"

Whoa, he knows our names!?

"Hiiiii!" Katie and I wave for the video, shocked by the sudden brush with stardom.

"You have no idea how this has made my day," Jason says, tucking the iPhone away. "Everyone is following your journey! And I was thinking maybe I'd run into you today, and then I saw packs at the junction and was like, it has to be you! And it is!"

"Well, you made our day too," I say, thankful our paths crossed with this kind and colorful soul.

"Really, I needed that unexpected boost of enthusiasm." Katie laughs.

"You got this!" Jason cheers and pumps his arms as he continues to the summit of Blake. "I'll see you on my way back down!"

A few minutes later, Jason gives us another dose of dancing and cheers as he runs past us on his way back down the mountain. "Go 46er ladies!"

"Hell yeah! Thanks, Jason!" I yell back at him.

As we complete our thirty-second High Peak, I swell with pride thinking of us as "the 46er ladies".

Nippletop (4,620 ft.) — No. 33
Dial Mountain (4,020 ft.) — No. 34

MINUTES TICK BY while I wait for Katie, sitting on my pack at the junction. The knot in my stomach tightens. A bold chipmunk darts around my feet, hoping I'll drop a few crumbs of the oatmeal raisin Clif bar I'm forcing myself to consume. As we reascended Colvin, Katie's limp had worsened, her leg so stiff she couldn't bend it at all. I gave her some space to work through it. But now she's slowing on the descents too. As the minutes spread out, fear wiggles itself into the spaces in between. I imagine that when she gets to the junction, she'll tell me she can't go on.

This might be it. I nervously tap my feet as I glance up the trail.

Roughly 125 miles, thirty-two High Peaks, nearly six days of movement. The closest I've come to finishing. But still two days from Whiteface and then the finish line. Sixty miles is not a hop, skip, and a jump away, especially when dealing with an injury. Maybe it's a sprain or a tear. Either one could end this attempt. There is one thing I know for certain: I won't go on without Katie. This isn't the same as when I wanted to stop in perfectly good health and come back for the overall record. In injury, we are tied to each other as partners. If it comes down to it, I will help evacuate her and it will be over—so close, yet so far.

A group of five hikers approaches me at the junction.

"Is this the way to Colvin and Blake?" one of the men asks me.

"Yeah, go right up that trail." I point the way I've just come down.

"Thank you." The group slowly begins to climb through the rock scrambles. Right as their last member rounds the bend, Katie comes into view, leaning on the trekking poles like a pair of crutches.

"Hey," I say cheerfully, trying to keep my tone upbeat. "How's the leg doing?"

"Fine." She moves past me and opens her pack.

Her short response surprises me. I just saw her hobble down the mountain while biting her lower lip to keep the pain inside. I'm pretty sure she's not fine, but I'm not sure how to address the elephant in the room.

"Katie…" I hesitate. "This seems pretty serious. I'm worried—"

"I'm going to finish." Katie cuts me off and her teary eyes meet mine. "I can do this."

"I know you can," I say. "But sometimes an injury stops us and it's out of our control. This thru-hike isn't worth permanently damaging your body."

Ultra distances can be like that. The consequence of pushing through can be a lifetime of chronic injury and pain. We don't know what's wrong with Katie's leg or whether it needs rest or medical attention.

"I can do this," Katie insists. "I know what my body can do. I've finally started believing I can do this. Like really, wholeheartedly believing. I'm not giving up now."

My head bows and I stare at my feet. Even though we've been on trail together for the last six days, Katie and I are still getting to know one another. It's hard for me to assess whether it's possible, or wise, for her to go on. I'm starting to worry that if she broke her ankle, she'd keep crawling. And if she gets really hurt, I feel like I would bear some of the responsibility for not convincing her to stop soon enough. But she's right; she knows what her body can do. I can't decide that for her.

"Okay," I say, weighing our options. This section of the route, near Keene Valley, has better cell phone service and more possible extraction points than most of what we have already traveled. "But let me take some of your pack weight," I insist.

"No, I'm fine," she says.

"It will help whatever you've got going on with your legs."

Katie doesn't respond.

"Please. Come on, Katie. This will help your leg."

"Okay." Katie reluctantly hands me the tent poles and some extra gear.

As we hike toward Nippletop, I'm still not sure we're making the right decision. But Katie is a grown woman, and I'm going to honor her choice to keep going, even if she's in pain. I need to trust that Katie knows her own limits. If I continue to worry about her, it will only take energy from the task at hand.

A little before noon, we reach the summit of Nippletop, the not-very-creative name for a mountain vaguely shaped like a breast. Some women have taken control of the narrative and made a statement by posing topless on the summit. For a moment, I think of stripping off my bra, but it's a little too cold for that, so I spread my arms wide.

Katie snaps a photo.

"It looks like you're hugging the Great Range." She holds the phone toward me so I can see. In the photo, my long bare arms wrap around the dome of Mount Marcy.

"Oh nice, I love it." I examine the photo before inquiring, "How are your legs feeling?"

"You know, they've loosened up a lot. Must be all the Tylenol and electrolytes."

With this positive turn of events, we leave the open summit to weave through pine forest, beginning the gentle one-mile ridgeline between Nippletop and Dial Mountain. Thick patches of sea green moss grow along the rutted trail. Through the trees, I catch glimpses of the Dix Range to our right and the Great Range to our left. In the midst of the mountains, I know I'm not far from my home in Keene. If we descended Dial and walked out to the road, I could be home in a few hours.

I wonder what Daniel is doing in my absence. And if he's staying sober. I always wonder.

Before us, the trail rises.

"Let's leave our packs here." I point to our right. "This is where the bushwhack starts."

We step off the trail and into the thick forest, dropping our packs among the pines. Dial Mountain is less than a quarter of a mile away, so we can scramble quickly up the last incline unburdened. Katie moves miraculously without a limp.

A pair of men in their sixties perch on the summit rock with their lunches spread before them. Trekking poles and packs lay to their sides.

"I think that's Haystack," one says from under the brow of his ball cap, pointing east.

"Hi there." I wave politely.

"Well, hello." They give us a friendly wave, happy to share the summit. "Sorry our gear is all over the place, we haven't come across many hikers."

"Oh, don't worry about that," Katie says.

We carefully maneuver to the highest point of Dial, from where we can look back to the Great Range.

Katie stretches her legs while I send out a group text. Before I turn off my phone, I see a new message from Daniel. *You're doing it.*

We are, I text back. I pause staring at the simple exchange, a warmth fluttering inside me. Daniel and I have hiked every one of these mountains together. There is no direction I can turn and not see or feel a memory of us. He has been with me since the clock started at Coreys Road. And he'll be with me until the clock stops. Maybe that's where it ends. I turn off my phone to save the 50 percent battery life I have remaining.

The men wish Katie and me a good day as we descend from the summit rock.

Within a few minutes, we are standing beside our packs again.

"I gotta pee," I say.

"Me too."

From behind our separate trees, I hear Katie squeal loudly. "Ah, this hurts."

"Oh, it does." I brace my back against a tree, so I only have to squat halfway. My thighs protest, screaming for it to be over. On the last day of my period, my pad only has a few spots of dried blood. A consolation prize to having my period during the thru-hike; my pads have been helpful in absorbing the last few drops of pee that never seem to shake off. Hitching my pants up, I tie them tightly around my belly button. With each passing day, my pants have grown baggier as my waist narrows and hunger grows. My insides grumble at the thought of food, and I try not to think about how quickly our supply is dwindling.

Dix Mountain (4,857 ft.) — No. 35

"Wʜᴀᴛ's ᴛʜᴇ ʙᴇᴀʀɪɴɢ?" Katie adjusts the compass.

"One twenty." I step in front of her.

Our plan for the Dial-to-Dix bushwhack is to follow the path of least resistance, descending through the forest until our paths cross the trail for Dix Mountain.

"If I get off course just holler left or right," I say.

"Okay."

To my left, I spot a V-shaped line through the conifer forest. Stabilizing my footing in the duffy earth, I grip mossy balsam trees. This place doesn't see many visitors. Brushing against the damp and earthy trees, I think of the last time I was here, In 2012, with Daniel and Jan. Looking for beta on this section of the thru-hike, I had reached out to Jan and he offered to guide us through.

"The bushwhack is quite simple," he'd explained as we picked our way through it, not even using a compass or GPS device. "It's almost impossible to mess up. You keep going down until you hit the streams, and you'll intersect the trail eventually."

After the hike, Daniel and I couldn't stop beaming about being on trail with Jan. *Jan.* Like *the* Jan. It felt like a torch had been passed to us, a blessing to repeat what he and Cory had accomplished.

But it wasn't meant for us, and I never thought it would take me eight years to get back to this place.

"Stay left!" Katie shouts from behind.

"Okay!" I scout a line to the left of a slick rock slab, which cuts down the mountain about forty feet. As we lose elevation, the forest opens up and navigation becomes quicker. Compared to other bushwhacks—where I've fallen in hidden holes, been slapped in the face by branches, or had claustrophobic breakdowns—this off-trail route is simple and straightforward. I dare say almost enjoyable, especially knowing Katie and I are shaving off over six miles by taking this shortcut.

"I hear water."

I spot the North Fork Boquet River. Large rocks provide footing across. After two more water crossings, I search for the dark swath of trail hidden somewhere ahead in the maple and birch forest. That's the thing about the dense Adirondack forest; you could be twenty feet from the trail and never know it was there.

"We're getting close," I sing to myself. "Getting close, getting close. Ah-ha! There!" My feet crash through patches of witch-hobble bushes and ferns before landing on the hard-packed trail.

"Woo-hoo!" Katie cheers and pockets the compass.

"Nice work," I say.

"You, too. That was smooth."

Being back on a cut trail feels like a dream, and my trail runners eat it up. Half a mile later, on the open slabs of the Dix slide, Katie and I take a break to refill our water bottles from a stream trickling down the rock.

"Probably a good idea to make our dinners before we get into the range," Katie suggests.

The Dix Range is notoriously dry, so we should utilize the water we have access to right now. Katie sets up the stove and I fill the pot. While the water boils, I lie back and listen to the stream as it cascades down the slide behind us. Slowly, I take deep breaths, in and out, relaxing and focusing my mind before our next mile, which will ascend 1,500 feet, one of the steepest miles on the route. I'm glad we were here recently on the Giant-Dix FKT, refamiliarizing ourselves with the technical terrain.

"We're going to take it slow," I assure Katie, sensing she's thinking about it too. She looks toward the massif of Dix Mountain, the sixth highest of the High Peaks.

Once our meals are hydrated, we pack up and Katie takes the lead. I pull out my earbuds and flip through playlists while Katie picks her way through the roots and rocks. As we scramble through the steepest pitches, I lighten the atmosphere by humming or singing aloud a favorite lyric to a favorite song. Katie looks back at me and laughs.

Roughly an hour later, approaching 4 p.m., the grade softens. Hardy bunchberries and blueberries grow along the summit ridge. Views begin to open, allowing the sun to shine directly in our eyes. We don our sunglasses as we crest the highest point. From the bare summit rock, we can see Lake Champlain sparkling in the distance and the Green Mountains of Vermont rising behind it.

"It's interesting," Katie says as we stretch our legs on the summit rock. "I was thinking about this on the ascent. There's a part of me that's like, 'I'm going to finish this hike at any cost.' And I have this powerful and stubborn confidence."

"Oh, I know!" I laugh. "You're the most stubborn person I know, and I'm pretty stubborn myself."

Katie looks off toward Elk Lake, before softly adding, "Then there's a part of me that wonders 'Who am I to be doing something like this?' And I question my ability. Every day, my mind keeps battling between the two."

"Katie, you are so strong, and you are doing this. Look at where we came from." I point toward the Seward Range, layers upon layers of mountains away.

"I know, but you make this look so easy."

"What do you mean?"

"It doesn't seem like this is challenging you at all."

"It is. Believe me, it is." I pause, thinking of all the fear and anxiety fighting for space in my mind. Living in a constant survival state. "If I make it look easy, it's because you're here with me," I say. "This was so much harder when I was by myself, and I would've bailed during or after that storm if you hadn't been with me. This is the farthest I've come. And you'll see, every ultra distance you do after this will be easier. You're just getting started."

"But your body isn't falling apart." Katie laughs and takes off her sunglasses to reveal her swollen face. "Look!"

"Oh jeez," I gasp, barely able to see her eyes. "Well, they're getting a little puffy, but we've got no one to impress out here."

Katie shakes her head and takes a long sip from her water bottle.

"You know, the week before the thru-hike, I had a lot of uncertainty about being able to complete this, so I called up one of my hiking mentors," she says, gazing out toward Elk Lake. "And she told me, you are you, and you are enough."

"I love that," I say, then add, "More than enough."

Hough Peak (4,400 ft.) — No. 36
South Dix (4,060 ft.) — No. 37
Macomb Mountain (4,405 ft.) — No. 38
Grace Peak (4,012 ft.) — No. 39

In the Dix Range, we flow from summit to summit. Hough Peak to South Dix, out-and-back to Macomb, back to South Dix, and then to Grace. The sky is hazy, the sun the deep orange of an egg yolk—because of wildfires burning out in the western US. By the time we reach the summit of Grace, our ninth and final peak for the day, the sun has set and small specks of green and blue lights outline the Champlain Valley. Headlamps hang around our necks, waiting for that moment where dusk turns to darkness.

"This one's for Grace," Katie says. A few days ago, she'd begun dedicating every summit to an individual who was important to her.

"For Grace," I agree.

Grace Hudowalski was the ninth person, but the first woman, to hike all 46 High Peaks. Her first round of the 46 began in 1922 at the age of sixteen with Mount Marcy and ended in 1935 with Esther Mountain. She then served as a vital member of the Adirondack 46ers Club, acting first as president and then secretary. During that time, she handwrote letters of encouragement to those aspiring to become 46ers and registered their journeys. In 2014, the mountain Katie and I now stand on was changed from East Dix to Grace Peak in her honor. Bringing the grand total of High Peaks bearing a woman's name to two: Grace Peak and Esther Mountain. And exactly like Grace, Katie and I will finish this round of 46 on Esther Mountain.

"Let's get to camp," I suggest, even though I really don't want to leave the sacred peak just as stars begin to emerge.

Katie sighs slowly, her breath visible. We descend into the pitch-black forest.

Navigating the herd path off Grace in the darkness is frustrating. Leading the descent, I lose the trail on the numerous stream crossings, doubling back across the softball-sized rocks and saying to Katie, "No, this way."

Finally, I see a large pool of pristine mountain water gathered at the base of a waterfall and know we're close. Daniel and I camped here long ago and spent the day lounging by the water and taking photos. I push the memory aside and locate the campsite.

"Oh, this is nice," Katie says.

"It's one of my favorites."

On our sixth night setting up camp, Katie and I are beyond proficient, barely speaking a word while we complete every task by the glow of our headlamps. Another cold night, nearly freezing. We wiggle into our sleeping bags and look at the photos from the day.

"I'll use my phone from here on out to take the summit photos," I say. "Save your battery for the big bushwhack tomorrow."

"Yep, powering down now." Katie tucks her phone into the warmth of her sleeping bag to help preserve the battery. After a moment of silence, she asks, "How does Daniel do with you being away for a week?"

"Uh, good. We're pretty used to spending time apart," I say. Thoughts of our separate rooms, separate beds, separate lives flutter in my mind. "I mean, we spent a lot of time as wilderness therapy instructors, and our work schedule was a week in the woods and then a week at home."

"Oh yeah, that makes sense."

The rustling of my sleeping bag fills my ears as I roll over. I wonder if I should tell Katie the truth—the woods are a sacred space to bear our souls after all. But what would she think if I told her Daniel and I have been separated for the past year? That he hid an alcohol addiction from me for several years? That I stayed with him, hoping we could get him the help he needed? Hoping I could get him back? That in the end it didn't turn out that way? That he'd told me he couldn't be a husband—couldn't be my husband? That I was furious for all the years I stayed? I wouldn't even know where to begin.

Instead I ask, "How's Kenny doing with you being gone for a week?"

"Not great," Katie says. "We don't spend a lot of time apart, and I know it's hard for him. Hard for me too."

"I hear ya." I empathize with Katie, if only in that I know what it is to be homesick. To miss the people you love. Years ago, Daniel had been someone I missed. I'd even sobbed, holding him close at JFK airport before I boarded a plane to India for four weeks. It had felt physically impossible to let him go.

Now that all seems like a memory belonging to a different person, a different couple. Maybe I'll tell Katie more tomorrow. Maybe I won't. There's so much I still don't understand. Like, why didn't he tell me he was struggling? I asked countless times, employing every wilderness therapy technique I knew, from journaling and couples therapy sessions to backpacking trips and reflective questions. We were best friends, and I didn't think we kept anything from each other. Obviously, I was wrong and that made me question everything I thought I knew. Not trusting the person you're married to is fatal for love. Perhaps I'll find the answers out here. But I doubt it.

Owls call in the distance. The South Fork Boquet River trickles by on a mission to meet up with the waters of the North Fork. Tomorrow we will rise and follow that water to New York State Route 73, where the final fifty miles await us. That is what I will focus on.

Day Seven

September 16, 2020
29.4 miles
11,000 feet vertical gain

Giant Mountain (4,627 ft.) — No. 40
Rocky Peak Ridge (4,420 ft.) — No. 41

ON THE SOUTH Fork Boquet River, our alarm sounds at 4 a.m. I brush away the crust from the corners of my eyes and knot my greasy hair into a bun. The bottoms of my feet ache and pulsate. I crawl from the tent on sore knees, and the brisk morning air offers my aching body some reprieve. I bring my left arm across my chest, stretching my stiff back and shoulder, then do the same for my right. Body odor escapes from my pits. There's no helping it at this point. Every article of clothing is encrusted in a layer of sweat and grime. Especially my socks. I'm not even sure if I'll wash them when I get home or throw them away.

Leaving camp, I hear another pair of owls call to each other. I pause midstride. "You hear that?"

Katie's footsteps stop too.

A few seconds pass in silence before the owl hoots again.

"Oh, that's my favorite sound out here," I say.

"Then it's a good sign."

Our first few miles are relatively flat, and Katie's pace is strong. I forget about the pain she was in yesterday at this time. The trail along the South Fork Boquet River weaves gently through maple and beech forests before meeting up with Route 73. On the paved road, we meet the dawn and sling our headlamps down around our necks. A semitruck drives past us, presumably headed to The Northway, a major four-lane highway that slices through the Adirondacks and connects to New York's Capital Region. Disputed from its conception, the highway undermined the idea of keeping the wilderness forever wild. Regardless, it was finally built in the 1960s and helped open the region to a whole new wave of tourism.

"I think that's the only car I've heard in seven days." Katie laughs. "Besides the ones creeping in and out of the Adirondack Loj parking lot on day three."

"It's definitely the first one we've heard at sixty miles an hour," I say. We hug the shoulder while another car speeds by. "Ah, they go so fast!"

For a week, Katie and I have been moving at the pace of the woods, an intentional movement that is neither fast nor slow yet consistent. The pace of the outside world is neither intentional nor consistent. Its short attention span is always wanting more. Maybe that's why I've always felt more at peace when I'm in the woods. Why being out here has always allowed me to take better care of my health, both mental and physical. And not just me—I've seen this so clearly in my wilderness students and Daniel too.

After two miles on the road, I'm itching to get away from the speeding cars, the smell of exhaust, and the ditches littered with beer cans and cigarette butts. I realize then that our encounter with Route 73 is a harbinger of the end. Our journey is almost complete. But I'm not ready to face the modern world—the messy reality of my life. I would like to slow down and stay out here longer. Or perhaps stand completely still. But this is a fantasy. The clock keeps ticking, and my body keeps moving forward.

Katie and I pause on the shoulder to check both directions for oncoming traffic before crossing the road and beginning the Ridge

Trail. My trail runners dig into the sandy soil as we start moving uphill, easing our road-cruising muscles back into mountain-climbing mode. About a mile up the trail, we stow our packs at an unused campsite near Washbowl Pond and load our daypack for Giant Mountain and Rocky Peak Ridge.

From the campsite, Katie picks her line up the rocky trail. I follow along behind. Half a mile later, views of the Dix Range open from the exposed ridgeline. The sun reaches down to warm our shoulders. A hint of humidity wafts in on the breeze. My mouth is dry, and I wonder if my one liter of water will be enough for the next seven miles, where there is no place to refill.

On the ridge, I look down to the glistening black waters of Chapel Pond and Giant's Washbowl. On the rocky, root-strewn shoreline of Chapel Pond, I have often shed my clothes to gingerly navigate the stones in only a pair of flip-flops. Even in the heat of the summer, I never stay in the water too long. It's icy cold and my body, especially my fingers, have difficulty rewarming. Even the memories of those swims cool me today, with the help of a gentle breeze that picks up as we near the summit of Giant.

As we climb, I follow the shadow of my younger self who first explored these ridgelines—barefoot and in a pink bikini top—with her little sister, yearning to show Mallory this new world she was discovering. I had marked our faces with streaks of brown mud and wore strings of shells and flowers around my ankles. It was my sister's first High Peak, and my sixth. We sat behind the summit rock and waited for a low bank of fog to clear before taking a picture on my disposable camera. The memory now lives in a photo album, tucked away in a dark corner of a trunk that I only open on occasion, whenever I have another journal or handful of photographs to stack onto the layers of my life.

"Ah!" A woman screams and I look up from following Katie's shoes.

"It's them! It's them!" A trio of college-aged women wearing SUNY Plattsburgh sweatshirts scream and leap up from the same rock where my sister and I took our photo years ago.

They run toward us and stop an arm's length away, respectful of COVID social distancing.

"Can we take a picture?" one woman asks. "I can't believe we're seeing you right now!"

"Of course," Katie replies.

We squeeze together, smiling for the multiple cameras. The moment feels surreal, like we are celebrities on a red carpet, but the carpet is muddy and our fancy outfits have been worn for seven days.

Behind the young women, Whiteface Mountain lies in the hazy distance.

"Number forty," I whisper to Katie.

"Oh my gosh!" She smiles. "Forty."

"Thank you for your support!" I say as we wave to the fan girls.

"You're so amazing!" They cheer as we backtrack a tenth of a mile to the junction for Rocky Peak Ridge.

Katie was right that day after the storm on Mount Marcy, when we were nestled in the col between Basin and Saddleback. It did matter that we finished this for women. For everyone. And for my younger barefoot self. For the twenty-three-year-old woman who graduated into the Great Recession and found a passion for climbing mountains. A young woman who didn't know what the future held but believed it could be something good. Something powerful. She focused on achieving a goal that had only been completed by two men, when she still feared her diagnoses would dictate her fate.

Maybe my future could still be good, even without Daniel. If I have the mountains, if I keep coming back to them, whatever I am going through, maybe I'll be okay.

On the descent, my feet pick their way through rocks and roots, making micro-decisions every second. My calves, quadriceps, and core tighten, transferring weight to the heels of my feet.

Rocky Peak Ridge is a little over a mile from Giant, a steep half-mile descent that loses seven hundred feet right off the bat. Seven hundred feet we'll have to reascend. These mountains are brutal and unforgiving. Gingerly, Katie lowers herself from slab to slab, using the trekking poles and her hands as much as possible. In the col between the two mountains, we cover a short distance of flat terrain, before climbing the five hundred feet to Rocky Peak Ridge.

Katie's gait stiffens and her pace drops. "I'm sorry I can't go faster."

"Katie, it's okay," I say.

I soak in the vibrant plant life around us as I match Katie's pace. There is little for me to complain about. My lungs work. I have no abdominal pain, and my legs are the strongest they've ever been. Thick mosses, bunchberries, and alpine flowers line the sides of the eroded trail. My favorite mountain flower, the color of indigo, reminds me of a small lupine—I don't even know its name. The irony of how much I still don't know despite all the time I've spent out here keeps my mind occupied for the next half hour.

On the summit, Katie and I sit beside a large pile of rock to stretch. It's almost 11 a.m.—the bluebird day only continues to warm. I'm down to half a liter of water. I take a few sips and munch on one of my last peanut butter and jelly wraps. To our right is the town of Keene Valley, and a little farther down Route 73 is Keene. My house. Daniel and Tahawus. Our prayer flags, our running shoes.

"Crazy to think we'll be sleeping in beds tomorrow night," I muse aloud.

"Seems unreal."

I pull out my phone to send a group update. *On the summit of*

Rocky Peak Ridge, #41. We will be finishing the thru-hike sometime tomorrow. After I hit send, I quickly power down my phone to stay in this world as long as I can.

Tomorrow. I'll be home tomorrow. But what was home to me at this point? Living downstairs while my husband lives upstairs. Waiting. Wondering. Anger. Mistrust. Hate. Love. Gut-wrenching sadness. Guilt. Numbness. And oddly enough, hope. Hope that one day I'll wake up and it will all be better.

The sun bakes down on Katie and me as we descend the exposed ridgeline to Washbowl Pond. Katie's pace is slower on the downhill. We've both run out of water. My cheeks are flushed, my fingers swollen and uncomfortable.

"I'm gonna run ahead, refill our water, and get it dropped," I say.

"Sounds good."

"I'll meet you at our packs." I scramble down the rocks with our empty daypack and enter the shade of the forest. In the sweetness of the pines, I stumble over a loose stone and catch myself against a tree trunk before more damage is done.

"Come on, Bethany," I mutter to myself. My mind has been elsewhere since the summit of Rocky Peak Ridge.

Down at the pond, I splash some water on my face. In the sandy shallows, it's lukewarm and does little to cool me. I fill our bottles, return to the campsite, retrieve our packs from behind a fallen tree, then put an iodine tab in each bottle.

While waiting for Katie, I lay all my gear on the logs around the fire pit to air out. On my ground pad I sit to open my bear canister. There isn't much left for thirty-five miles, give or take. One of Katie's homemade dehydrated meals, one Clif bar, one cup of peanut butter, one Tailwind packet, one peanut butter and jelly wrap, and a small bag of nuts. My body wants more. I look up the trail—still no sign of Katie. On top of the shrinking food supply lies the uncertainty of how quickly we'll cover the remaining miles with Katie's injury, which has flared up again. Making it all the more difficult to ration.

"Come on, Katie," I mumble, not wanting to wait anymore on this increasingly hot afternoon.

Waiting makes too much space for all the things I've been holding back. Anger, frustration, sadness. The thought of going home tomorrow makes me nauseous.

About five months ago, shortly after the COVID-19 pandemic began, Daniel and I went for a walk down to the Ausable River to break up the monotony of working from home. Spring was budding and pushing out the river's ice. Tahawus pranced in front of us on his leash, a spark of joy in dark times. I was grateful we had all gotten out together for a walk.

That is when Daniel said, "I think we need to separate."

"What?" I stopped.

"I don't think I can be a husband anymore. I just . . . it's just . . . I'm really struggling to even take care of myself."

"I know." I stumbled over my words, trying to control my anger. "But why now? I've been talking to you about this for years. Asking if you're okay, asking if we would be better apart."

Daniel looked out at the river. Silent. Scared. He had been sober for eleven months but seemed to be sinking more than ever.

"And you always wanted to stay together, and I stayed with you, through all of this. And now you're telling me you can't be my husband?"

"I'm so sorry, Bethany. You don't deserve this."

"Oh, I know you're sorry, you're always sorry, and you never wanted to hurt me. But guess what? All your silence, all the times you should have told me what was going on, all these years that have gone by . . ." I yelled, so incredibly angry I had ever married this person and trusted him to protect me. To support me. That I had tried to help him over and over and this was how he repaid me. Daniel's thin frame curled away from me. He had no words to offer. No comfort to give. Once again failing me. "You know what? I can't do this anymore. I should have left years ago, but I didn't because you still wanted to make this work. But you knew this wasn't working, and I knew this wasn't working. You just weren't brave enough to do the hard thing."

Neither was I. And now I was trapped with him in a pandemic. For better or worse.

A month later, Daniel's mental health began to spiral even further. I tried to provide as much support as I could muster from a position of separation. Rain poured from the night sky.

He walked into the living room, hands trembling. "I have to get out of here. I need to go for a drive or something."

"Be careful," I said, uncomfortable with the thought of him driving. But at that point, I was uncomfortable with the idea of him being anywhere—I could almost feel him trying to crawl out of his own skin.

"I will."

Thirty minutes later, my phone rang.

"I'm sorry." He cried, his voice cutting in and out. "Bethany, I'm so sorry."

My hands grew clammy, and my heart pounded in my ears. This was it. This was the moment he'd chosen to end his life, and this was his goodbye call. Where he'd tell me how much he loved me, but he simply couldn't do it anymore. That I'd be better off without him.

"Daniel, where are you?" I bolted toward the door, grabbing my purse and car keys, imagining him on a high cliff leaning forward. "Dan!"

His voice broke through my frantic questioning. "The car, I'm so sorry. I got in an accident."

"What?" I placed a hand on the top of my head, heart throbbing, feet pacing. "Are you okay?"

"I'm okay, but the car—it's totaled. I'm sorry, I'm so sorry." Daniel sobbed. "I lost control and it hit the guard rail."

"Ah, don't worry about the car." I exhaled. "I'm just glad you're okay. Where are you?"

"Cascade Pass." His voice was small and far away. "I'm so sorry about everything, about everything Bethany."

"I know," I said. "I know."

I drove to where the inky black waters of Cascade Lake nestled between two sheer slopes of rock. I knew Daniel was sorry. The lies, the life we'd dreamed of but been unable to build. For the pain his addiction caused the one person he loved most. He was his toughest critic. That's why as I pulled up behind the totaled car, I wondered if it had really been an accident. Or maybe he had tried to drive his car into the lake.

"I thought about it," he admitted later that night. "But as soon as I hit the guardrail, I knew I wanted to live."

Even after he told me he couldn't be my husband, I didn't move out. I was still too scared he wouldn't survive without me in his fragile state. Looking at the mangled car, it hit me, like an ice jam breaking: It was actually our being together that made it harder for us to survive. And if we didn't get out soon, it could be fatal.

My cheeks are flushed with heat and emotion when I hear Katie's shoes scuffing against the trail. Her maroon shirt and blue buff come into view.

"Hey!" Katie smiles.

"Hey," I say, grabbing my socks and shoes, ready to move away from my anger. "I got our waters."

"Thanks." Katie sits on a log by her pack. "Sorry about my pace. I felt better this morning, then that downhill really tore up my legs again."

"Our food is getting pretty low, so we should probably get moving in a few minutes," I say. "I want to try to hit the bushwhack in the light." I continue to focus on the business at hand, knowing our chances of getting to the bushwhack before nightfall are slim. It's already after 1 p.m.—we only have five or six hours of daylight remaining and Big Slide Mountain is still ten miles away. But logistics are a welcome distraction from my inner thoughts.

Katie nods and bites her lower lip. "I'm really sorry I'm slowing us down."

"We're doing fine. We just have to keep moving." I push gear into my pack. It's easy to forget that while I was waiting and resting and overthinking, Katie was working to get here and probably chastising herself about being too slow.

"Hey . . ." My voice softens. "I'm sorry. I was sitting around and worrying. And the heat, I hate the heat." I attempt to transfer my real frustration onto nature. To do anything to not have to explain what's going on in my head. But Katie's energy doesn't rebound, and all I've done is taken my anger and put it somewhere it doesn't belong. I'm not the only one going through something. But when my mind gets fuzzy, that's the first thing I forget. It's so easy to feel bitterly sorry for myself.

"Five mountains to go," I say, trying to make the miles we still have to cover seem small and tangible.

Katie nods and reassembles her pack, but I can tell my attitude has hit her most vulnerable place. I can feel her questioning herself and her ability as if waves of doubt are emanating from her body. Fuck. Hurt people hurt people. It's true but it's not an excuse. I'm full of regret. In silence, we clip into our packs and hike forward, both of us battling our demons as the afternoon heat rises in the valley.

Big Slide Mountain (4,240 ft.) — No. 42

WE ENTER THE town of Keene Valley walking single file down the shoulder of Route 73 and begin the slow ascent to the garden parking lot.

When Katie and I are finally able to walk side by side, I apologize. "Hey, I'm sorry about earlier."

"It's okay, I get it. Waiting in the heat isn't fun."

"Well, it's more than that . . ." I pause, searching for words though I've been thinking of what to say for the better part of an hour. "Just being in this area and getting so close to the finish—I've been thinking a lot about going home tomorrow. And recently things haven't been great between Daniel and me."

"Really?"

"Yeah, and I tried to downplay it so you wouldn't think I'd be distracted out here."

"I get that," Katie admits. "It really frustrates me when I appear weak, like with my legs. But I'm sorry about you and Daniel. That must be painful. I hope it works out."

"Yeah, me too," I say.

While Katie might mean she hopes it works out and we stay together, I have a growing intuition that it will work out and I'll be starting my life anew. And I'm sure in the future as our friendship grows, I'll tell her the full story. But for now, this is enough.

The air cools as we climb out of the valley and back into the mountains. We stop at the first stream crossing we come to. The water, which normally runs much stronger, is stagnant and murky, littered with decaying leaves.

"I think this is going to be our only water on Big Slide," I say, scouting for the cleanest section.

We crouch by the water source, using our hands to scoop out the leaves and create a small bowl from which we can fill our bottles. An owl hoots in the distance.

"Did you hear that?" I ask, swiveling my head upward.

Just after four in the afternoon, a couple of hours of daylight remain. Perhaps I'll finally see the creature whose voice has provided the soundtrack to our most recent days.

"Yes!" Katie exclaims.

We hold our breath, waiting for another owl to reply.

Hoot-hoo-hoo-hooo, hoot-hoo-hoo-hooo.

"Who cooks for you? Who cooks for you?" I mimic back. "I think it's a Barred Owl."

"Oh cool."

"Another good sign," I say. "You know, owls starting our day and being with us now."

"They're hooting us on," Katie jokes.

"Oh my gosh." I giggle at her G-rated punchline as I drop an iodine tab into my water bottle and shake it back and forth.

Listening to the owls, we share a few bites of our last dehydrated meal, completely immersed in our here and now.

Surprisingly, the long ascent is peaceful and almost relaxing. Owls continue their dusk calls, and although I never see one, I find joy in their company. In our flow state, Katie's legs move more fluidly. The hazy sky hangs over as we gain 3,200 feet over the next four miles, ascending up and over The Brothers, three smaller mountains leading up to Big Slide. A garter snake slithers into the crevice of a rock. About a mile from the summit, we leave our full packs in the col where we'll return to begin the bushwhack. Wearing our headlamps like necklaces, we make the top of Big Slide before sundown. Katie spreads out the 46Climbs bandana on the summit rock and takes a picture.

To the west, the sun lowers over the shoulders of Mount Marcy and the rock face of Big Slide falls sharply to Johns Brook Valley. It's like we're sitting on the edge of the world. For a moment we linger in silence, absorbing the transformative energy between night and day.

"Well, we should probably get going." I sigh.

Katie nods and we scramble down. At our packs, we take a few minutes to compose ourselves in the growing darkness for the mile-and-a-half bushwhack to Porter Mountain. To me, this is the crux of the thru-hike—the last challenge. Once we complete it, we're officially in the homestretch. From the beginning of our scouting missions, Katie and I agreed she would lead this, the biggest navigational piece of the whole thru-hike because of her strong background in and love for off-trail travel.

"Can you take these?" Katie asks, passing me the trekking poles.

"Of course," I say, knowing she'll need her hands free to steady the map on her phone. Throughout our adventure, Katie has protected her phone's battery life for this very moment. When scouting the thru-hike, we completed this same bushwhack on a humid August day. While Katie set our course and took notes, I munched on blackberries and raspberries, taking a back seat and completely trusting in her as a partner. From the beginning, we had leaned on my knowledge and experience for planning because I had already attempted the route twice. Delegating the bushwhacks to Katie was the first step in making our endeavor feel like a team effort.

She adjusts her headlamp and takes a deep breath. Between us and the summit of Porter Mountain are some impassable boggy areas that we'll have to navigate around.

The crux begins.

Porter Mountain (4,059 ft.) — No. 43
Cascade Mountain (4,098 ft.) — No. 44

KATIE WEAVES INTO the woods, slowly and deliberately. We tread lightly over the soft, duffy terrain. She stops often, studies the map, and makes slight adjustments to her course. I follow her faithfully—navigating is her skill set. A warm wind blows through the treetops and white moths flutter around our headlamps, like little angels. Every now and then, I pause behind Katie, simply admiring her strength. A moth lands on my shoulder, and I study its powdery body. It stays attached to me for a few steps before floating away into the shadows of the forest. The moths, the sweet-smelling wind, Katie's breath, it all becomes a meditation and minutes slip by.

More than an hour into the bushwhack, Katie stumbles in the dark and braces herself on a tree limb, her body and mind fatigued. For a moment, I think of offering to take point, but hold back. We are so close to the main trail—she's gotten us almost all the way there.

I remember leading my younger sister, Mallory, on an unintentional bushwhack toward the summit of Mount Marshall on her last hike before becoming a 46er. We had somehow veered off the main herd path to another smaller path, which eventually petered out. Instead of turning back, I set a bearing with my compass and pushed upward through thick trees.

"Are we lost?" Mallory cried, not accustomed to the claustrophobic nature of bushwhacking, the art of traveling off trail with a map and compass. Her breathing became shallow and panicky as she pushed through tangled branches.

"No, no. We aren't lost." I tried to comfort her. "I have a bearing."

When we finally reunited with the trail a few hundred yards from the summit, sweaty and scratched, with leaves in our hair, she fell to her knees and pressed her lips to the dark, compacted mud.

"Let's take a break," I say to Katie, realizing we haven't eaten or drunk anything since beginning the bushwhack. I've been in a trancelike state, floating along behind without a thought to maintaining our bodies during these miles.

"But we're almost to the trail," Katie says, looking at her phone.

"I know, but this is a nice place for a little break," I say, gesturing to the grassy meadow we are skirting around. Birch trees surround us, their white bark glowing in the night. "Let's finish our dinner here."

"I'm not hungry."

"Just a little something." I sit on a fallen log.

"But I want to get to the trail. We're so close."

"And eating and hydrating will help us get there in one piece." I give her a pointed look from my position on the log. I've accepted that she is going to be pushing herself through pain for the remainder of the hike. I can at least make sure she's doing what she can to stay safe: eating, drinking, and taking pain medication. "Plus, your shoe is untied."

Katie finally surrenders to her untied shoe and sits down on the log beside me.

I pull out the last, partially eaten Thanksgiving dinner. Mashed potatoes coat the inside of the plastic bag. I take a bite before passing it to Katie.

"Thanks." She nods.

The sight of the mushy food isn't appealing, but every calorie counts, so when Katie passes the bag back to me, I lick it clean. My shoelaces have also come loose from the bushwhack—the undergrowth grabbing and pulling at us while we marched through.

"Okay, you were right in making me stop," Katie admits, no longer looking like a zombie on autopilot. "We were just so close to the trail, and I want this bushwhack to be over with."

"I know," I agree. "I've been guilty of that too. Many times."

"Thanks for looking out for me," she says.

"Of course," I say, knowing at this moment, our world consists of nothing more than being there for each other.

When our feet land on the compact dirt trail, we both sigh deeply.

"Beautiful, beautiful maintained trail. There you are." I pass the trekking poles back to Katie.

"If my legs didn't hurt so much, I'd kneel down and kiss it," Katie adds.

I think of my little sister kissing the trail to Mount Marshall and exclaiming her thanks to God over and over again.

The bushwhack is done. The last major piece of the puzzle between us and the end of the thru-hike is complete. On the summit of Porter, we pause briefly to take a photo, then continue on to Cascade Mountain. Compared to the unknowns of the bushwhack, this trail is familiar to me; it's like walking down the road I grew up on. In the glow of my headlamp, I recognize features I've journeyed past countless times, like the Y-shaped balsam tree I always use to stabilize myself through choppy downclimbs and the rock that looks like a heart.

At the junction, Katie and I drop our full packs, put on an extra layer, and pocket our phones for the quick half-mile round trip to the summit of Cascade Mountain. A warm wind blows above the treeline. Below us, the lights from the town of Lake Placid twinkle. We are so close to the modern world, yet still far away. My jacket flaps in the wind and I smile. There's nothing I love more than being high on a mountain in the darkness of night with the stars above me. It's pure freedom. Near midnight, Katie and I hug on the summit.

"Two more," I cheer and squeeze her shoulders. "Do you believe in miracles? Do you believe in miracles?"

Katie laughs at my reference to *Miracle on Ice*, which recalls what happened right here in Lake Placid when the United States hockey team beat the Soviet Union during the 1980 Olympics. She adds, "I don't know where you get your night energy from."

"From the mountains," I sing into the miraculous black of midnight. "From the wind!"

On the descent, my exuberant mood is tempered by my legs, which begin to ache in ways I've never experienced on trail. Hot jabs of pain radiate from my knees and travel up my thighs. I wince and bite down on my lower lip, debating whether Katie and I should now split the trekking poles. Another bolt of pain removes my hesitation.

"Uh, can I get one of those trekking poles?" I ask Katie at the junction, before we shoulder our full packs.

"Of course." Katie hands me a pole. "I wondered when the descent pain would hit you."

"Oh, it's here."

Each armed with one pole, we hobble down Cascade for two miles and crazily laugh off the pain of forty-four High Peaks. We refill our empty bottles at a large stream and occasionally hear a car passing on Route 73 less than a quarter mile away.

"We should probably camp here." I point to a flattish section of hardwoods to our left. "Once we get on the road, there won't be an easy place to pull over and sleep."

"Should we bother setting up the tent?" Katie asks. "Or sleep under the stars?"

"I'm all for the stars."

Away from the main trail, we tuck ourselves beneath a large maple tree and curl up for three hours of sleep. Now that we're in the homestretch, sleep is a luxury we can cut back on.

Lying on my back, I look up at the dark leaves. *Today is the day. Today, we'll finish what we started. What I've started twice before. What started nearly ten years ago . . .* My eyes close and the earth rocks me to sleep.

Day Eight

September 17, 2020
21.2 miles
4,400 feet vertical gain

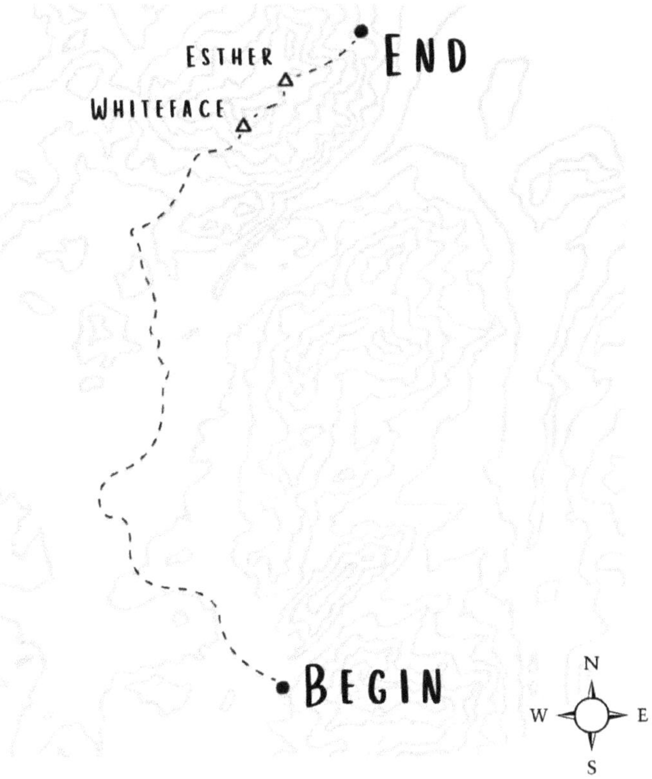

Whiteface Mountain (4,867 ft.) — No. 45

BEFORE THE ALARM sounds, I'm awake and taking in the indigo shades of 3:30 a.m. *Have I even slept?* I feel as if I just blinked. Even though our finish point is still more than twenty miles away, I can envision it vividly. In my sleeping bag, I wiggle my toes and feel the discomfort of my taped blister. Katie rolls to her side.

"Good morning." She coughs, her lungs adjusting to the predawn air. "Did you sleep?"

"I guess," I say. "How about you?"

"A little. My legs are pretty stiff."

From inside my sleeping bag, I take out my headlamp and click it on. The light bounces around the dark green undergrowth. Barefoot, I retrieve my bear canister and change into my mud-crusted pants, drawing the waist as tight as I can. For the last time, my sleeping polypro top comes off, and I shove my arms through my sports bra. Back at my sleeping bag, I sit on my ground pad and use my hands to brush leaves from the bottom of my feet. The crevices between my toes are stained dark brown. I wrap one more piece of Leukotape around my blister.

"Just think, we're gonna be able to take showers tonight."

"That sounds amazing," Katie says.

The remainder of my food fits neatly into one small ziplock bag. For the last twenty miles, I have one packet of caffeinated Tailwind, one energy bar, and one peanut butter and jelly wrap to sustain me. The energy bar will get me going this morning, then I'll have the Tailwind, and I'll save the wrap until Whiteface and Esther. I'll drink lots of water. Having a plan helps soothe the emptiness in my stomach. I try not to think about all the food waiting for me as soon as we get back to civilization. I load all the dirty laundry and gear I won't need during the day into my now-empty bear canister and clamp the lid shut.

With my pack clipped into place, I marvel at its lightness, feeling like I could run to the finish line.

"I'm a horse returning to the stables." I laugh, lacing my hands under my shoulder straps and trotting a few steps to the main trail, feeling silly and unburdened. Katie shakes her head and giggles.

Young saplings brush against our shins as we make our way back to the packed trail. Within a few minutes, Katie and I emerge onto the shoulder of Route 73 and head north toward Lake Placid.

The road is quiet. That's the magic of 4 a.m. The time my father always started his days on the farm. As a child, I loved to look out my bedroom window at the warm light pouring from the square barn windows. We pass the turnoff for the Mount Van Hoevenberg Olympic Bobsled Run as we climb upward. After two hours and five miles of road walking, we take a right off Route 73 onto Jackrabbit Trail, a forty-mile ski trail that runs from Paul Smith's College to Keene. In the blueish pre-dawn light, we hydrate and I eat half of my energy bar. This part of the Jackrabbit Trail runs through a golf course, and on the dewy manicured lawn, I power up my phone to send a quick text to the group chat. *On trail. Should be to the finish around one or two.* At 8 percent, the battery is red.

"How much battery is left on your phone?" I ask Katie.

"About twenty percent."

"Cool, can we plan to use yours for the last two summit photos?" I ask. "Mine might not make it."

"Sure," Katie says, then looks at me with a serious face. "Be honest, how puffy are my eyes?"

Katie's eyes disappear behind her bloated cheeks, a common side effect of ultra distances, when your body is unable to flush everything out and you begin to swell. "Um, well, maybe wear sunglasses for the photos," I stammer. We both laugh. "You look beautiful."

"Yes, we are both stunning," Katie agrees.

"Dirt looks good on us."

"And scrapes and bruises," she adds.

The morning fog lifts, but the sky remains overcast as Katie and I cross the golf course. We are delivered onto River Road after a gentle walk through hardwood forest. Horses graze in open pastures that border the mountainous landscape. We walk single file along the sandy shoulder of the winding yet predominantly flat road. We stop to put on our shells as a light rain begins to fall. The sprinkle comes and goes, but neither Katie nor I worry about it. It's refreshing. Spritzing us with life and energy.

By the time we reach the trail register at Whiteface Landing, the gray sky is brightening. Roughly ten miles remain. I wonder who will be waiting for us at the Atmospheric Sciences Research Center (ASRC) parking lot. If it weren't for the pandemic, I'm sure lots of my family would have made the trip, like they had planned to do in 2016.

The trail ascends a small hill and Katie's gait changes, stiffening at the knees. I know at this point, nothing will keep her or me from the finish. I begin thinking about the concept of not giving up. If I divorce Daniel, am I giving up on my marriage? Is it a failure if we go our own ways, even if it saves our lives? Will I ever forgive him? Or better yet, myself? And at the end of the day, which decision is the right one? Is there even a right one?

At the Whiteface Lean-to, I take a few bites of my peanut butter and jelly wrap. The last packet of Tailwind is in my water bottle. I shake it up and down. As I pack away my wrap, my stomach grumbles for more. I promise myself I can have the rest when we make the summit of Whiteface: two miles and over two thousand feet of intense elevation gain away.

"Just take it slow," I tell Katie when the rolling trail becomes a steep incline. Huge boulders stand in our way, and I can tell she's struggling to bend her knees. She stops, drops, and crawls over the large rocks.

"Go ahead," she says when she is back on her feet, pausing and leaning hard against the trekking poles.

"You sure?" I can see that she is deep in the pain cave.

"Yeah."

"Okay, I'll see you up there."

Within a few minutes we are out of each other's sight. An unrelenting staircase of stones ascends sharply, weaving through gnarly pine and birch trees. I slow my pace even more and put in my earbuds. Thankfully, this is the last challenging ascent. Once we hit the summit of Whiteface, the fifth highest mountain in the 46 High Peaks, we'll descend a ridgeline to Esther, then turn on a somewhat gentler out-and-back without much elevation gain.

I scramble over and through boulders until I pop out above the treeline, but there's no view. Only a humid fog. Near the summit, I hunker down amid a pile of rocks and put on my rain jacket to block the breeze. Minutes go by without any sign of Katie. But her absence doesn't make me uneasy; come hell or high water, I know she'll join me on this summit.

From my pack I pull out my phone and food bag. While my phone powers up, I take a few bites of my wrap. It's almost noon.

On Whiteface, I message Daniel outside of the group chat. I know he'll be at the finish line with his camera. The text sends and the screen goes black.

"Well, that's that," I sigh, returning my phone to the worn ziplock baggie I've been keeping it in to protect it from moisture. Then my MP3 player dies. Another sign our journey is swiftly coming to an end.

And here I am. In the fog, nestling against the same triangular mountain I've been catching glimpses of all week, that I sketched next to numerous itineraries in countless notebooks as four years turned to eight, turned to eleven. The mountain that once seemed impossibly far away. The mountain that kept calling me back again and again—telling me to become the first woman to hike all 46 High Peaks unsupported. But it won't just be me. And I'm proud of that, because putting two women's names on the board is better than one. I am not an anomaly, an exception to the rule. Women are strong—each of us in our own way. Katie and I faced different challenges, and we are both going to finish.

As if on cue, Katie emerges through the fog.

"You waited for me," she says.

"Of course." I push myself to a standing position. "We have to go to the summit together."

Side by side, we continue climbing, eventually stopping at the jagged white summit sign marking the elevation at 4,867 feet. Together we sit on the summit, and I throw up my hands while Katie snaps the photo.

"Whiteface." I beam. "We made it!"

"Even if I had to crawl a bit." Katie laughs.

"Let's pop our extra-strength Tylenol," I suggest.

"Yes! Let me dig those out of my pack."

I take a few sips from my water bottle, mindful to conserve my remaining liter of Tailwind for the six mostly downhill miles that remain.

"Here." Katie passes me a white pain pill.

"Thanks." I pop it into my mouth. "Can I get a trekking pole too?"

She pushes the pole in my direction. I take a deep breath, not looking forward to the painful descent but knowing it's the only way to go.

Esther Mountain (4,240 ft.) — No. 46

ALONG THE RIDGELINE, the Whiteface Veterans' Memorial Highway snakes through the fog. The road was built in the '30s to honor those lost to the First World War. Constructed during the Great Depression, it helped create jobs in the Adirondacks. It was heavily supported by Franklin D. Roosevelt, who also saw the road as an accessible way for persons of all abilities to experience the beauty of the mountains. The road brings visitors to a parking area a quarter mile below the summit of Whiteface, from which they can reach the top by way of an elevator installed inside the mountain. How I would love a magical elevator to transport me to Esther right about now.

We tenderly pick our way down the loose rocks and pass over the truck trail that connects to the Whiteface ski trails. In the col between Whiteface and Esther, the trail flattens so Katie and I can elongate our strides. Then in the center of the trail, a large pile of rocks marks the herd path for Esther Mountain—our final High Peak. It feels surreal. We place our packs to the side of the trail for the last time.

"Well, shall we go visit our good friend Esther?" I ask.

"I think it's time." Katie grins.

We pack the daypack with the sparse remainder of our food and water. I swipe my fingertips against the charcoal earth and mark my cheekbones with it. Now I'm ready. On the one mile out to Esther, Katie and I don't talk much. We cover the ground quickly as the extra-strength Tylenol kicks in with full force. My trail runners navigate patches of mud, but at this point, I'm not as picky about my footing as I was in the swamps of the Seward Range on day one. Every now and then, muddy water seeps between my toes.

The trail dips gently and crosses a swampy area with the aid of wooden planks. Gradually we weave upward through the shrubby forest and pass over the false summit. A rock slab replaces the dark brown earth. At the end of the trail is the bronze plaque that honors the indomitable spirit of Esther McComb, who first ascended the mountain in 1839 at the age of fifteen. One hundred years after her ascent, a group of hikers including the first female 46er, Grace Hudowalski, climbed to the summit to install a plaque here in Esther's honor.

"Hi, Esther." I kneel beside the plaque, brushing pine needles away from the emblazoned script. *Esther McComb, Age 15, Who made the first recorded ascent of this peak for the sheer joy of climbing.*

"Forty-six," Katie says.

"Forty-six."

The moment feels like everything I imagined it would. For nearly a decade, I've envisioned getting to this point, battered and bruised with mud on my face.

"We have to get a photo like Cory and Jan did!" I lie down on my side next to the plaque and prop myself up with an elbow, imitating the newspaper picture that started this whole quest.

Katie powers up her phone and pats the top of her head. "Oh no, I forgot my sunglasses." She sighs and snaps the selfie. Checking the image, her puffy eyes widen ever so slightly. "Oh my gosh, you can hardly see my eyes!"

"Here, you can borrow mine." I pass her my pink shades.

"Thanks." She puts them on. "I want to get a nice photo with the 46Climbs bandana."

Grabbing the bandana from her pack, Katie's body stiffens for a moment. Behind the shades, tears fall. Watching her, I choke up, thinking about everything that has led us to this moment. Those things that make us never the same. It's the mountains that support us during those times and give us hope that maybe we can survive. Not only survive, but maybe even be fortunate enough to understand our pain and make peace with it. To understand that life is loss. And loss is life. To let go.

"We did it, Katie." I snap the photo.

"Yes, we did."

As powerful as this moment is, we cannot linger for too long. Even though this is our last summit, the clock doesn't stop until we reach the trailhead and parking lot: still roughly three and a half miles away. I offer my hand to Katie and help her to a standing position. My fingers are swollen and only a few remnants of blue nail polish remain on the tips of my nails.

"To Esther and Grace and all the badass mountain women of the world," I say, embracing Katie in a bear hug.

"Here, here," Katie echoes. "To Esther and Grace."

"Let's go tell the world we made history."

The final mile descent off Esther Mountain is brutally steep. I bite down on my lower lip to keep from whimpering. Katie and I both hobble down the path, crutching ourselves with a single trekking pole. We are so close, yet in so much pain. With each step, our muscles scream, "Please let this be done." Our food is gone. Water too. Birch and aspen trees line the trail with more orange and yellow leaves than when Katie and I began our journey a week ago.

"It's them!" A voice calls in the distance.

Looking down the trail, I don't see anyone, but then I hear a second whoop and a dog barking. My dog.

"Tahawus!" I yell, instantly distracted from my burning fatigue.

Tahawus yips and bounces around my legs. I scoop all thirteen pounds of his terrier furriness into my arms, as he enthusiastically licks my cheeks.

"Oh, my buddy! I've missed you." I burrow my face into his fur.

He barks and wiggles until I set him down so he can run around my feet. Around the bend is Daniel—camera in hand. He stands at the side of the trail, snapping photos of Katie and me. From the trail, I bend over and pick up an orange aspen leaf. Before we crest the final steps and join the group of family and friends waiting for us in the parking lot at the end of the trail, I pause next to Daniel.

"Happy early birthday." I pass him the leaf, thinking of the first birthday card I ever made him, out of birch bark and maple leaves, while we were wilderness therapy instructors. He loved the card so much that we promised to each other right then and there that we would never buy a gift for each other. This will probably be the last birthday I'll celebrate with him. "Thank you," he says.

I step back from Daniel, and the movement makes me think of something a marriage counselor had told me early in our separation. "Right now, you have one foot in your marriage and one foot out. But you can't stay like that forever. A moment will come when you will know."

"Know what exactly?" I'd asked, dabbing my tears with a tissue.

"Where to put that other foot. In or out. You can only live in two worlds for so long."

That moment had come this summer on the Fourth of July. Daniel and I were in Cherry Valley celebrating my grandfather's eighty-first birthday. Besides my parents and sisters, no one knew we were separated and my family kept asking about him.

"Why don't you drive down for the party?" I'd suggested, hoping the family gathering might make us reconsider our separation. Or maybe it would confirm it.

From my parent's house, we'd chosen to walk the three miles through the woods. I'd traveled this way a thousand times as a child, going to work on my grandparent's vegetable farm in the summer. As we were walking Daniel told me, "My sister's pregnant."

"Oh my gosh." I inhaled joy and exhaled sorrow. Stopping in the middle of the white birch and hemlock forest I felt my vision blur, but my intuition cleared. In a choked voice, I asked, even though it was more of a statement, "That's never going to be us, is it?"

"No." Daniel shook his head and reached for my hand.

Under the trees we hugged and cried for everything we had once believed we would have and everything we were losing. When I stepped away from him, my feet finally aligned outside of our marriage.

That night a full moon rose over the valley, its light too bright for any stars to shine.

Up there somewhere in the blackness were Cassiopeia and Orion, scattered remnants of a honeymoon dream that never got to be born. I mourned the young couple who once lay on Duck Hole Dam looking at the night sky before the hurricane arrived. Oh, what the flood would bring.

Daniel smiles at me, just like he did on our first hike together. He's beaming as he focuses the lens on Katie and me.

"Thanks for being here," I say with earnest appreciation, knowing that even though this is a happy moment, it is the beginning of a painful goodbye. Someday we'll sign a stack of papers in a lawyer's office and become strangers to one another.

"I wouldn't miss it," he says from behind the camera. His

finger clicks down again and again, snapping a series of photos. Looking back at him, I wonder if he yearns for a world that is more accepting of his emotional struggles as a man, just as I long for one that doesn't question my physical strength as a woman. What a just world that would be.

He steps to the side, so Katie and I can continue forward.

The small crowd assembled at the trailhead hoots, hollers, and claps. Katie's black lab mix runs to her, tail wagging. "Hey, bub!" She smiles.

Side by side, Katie and I take the final step, and I plant my hiking pole into the ground. The clock stops. It's over.

"What time is it?" I ask Katie.

"3:05," she says.

I calculate slowly. "Seven days, four hours, and fifty minutes."

We have beaten the original record set by Cory and Jan in 2009 but missed the overall record currently held by Michael, Paul, and Dan by twenty-three hours. In this moment there is absolutely no regret, or energy for it. We are here to celebrate. The storm hit, we tried to keep going, we couldn't, we waited, we stayed in it. And for the first time, two women are standing at the finish line, having thru-hiked all 46 High Peaks unsupported.

"I have gifts for you!" Kenny runs over to the trunk of his car. He opens it to reveal cardboard boxes filled with loaves of bread, bottles of red wine, sandwiches, and sports drinks.

"What do you want?" He gives me a big hug. "I'm so proud of the two of you!"

"Ah, thanks Kenny," I say, peering over his shoulder at the food. "Let's try that bread."

"You got it!" Kenny passes Katie and me each a warm loaf from a local bakery.

The feast is overwhelming. No longer do I have to think about rationing my food. After a few bites of the bread, I return to the small crowd and talk with friends from the hiking community. Surprisingly, I'm not as hungry as I had been that morning. The rumble in my stomach has been replaced by surging adrenaline. Katie and I pose for pictures and smile with our sunglasses on, hiding our puffy, sleep-deprived eyes.

"Thank you for coming out," I say to the crowd, which has spread out in true COVID fashion. Even so, it doesn't detract from the genuine enthusiasm and wonder for what we have accomplished. A group of my freshman students from Paul Smith's College, who've been tracking our progress from the first day, stand in a horseshoe shape cheering and waving two homemade signs. "Congratulations Katie and Bethany!" "Herstory made!"

We pose and smile, pose and smile.

"Alright, I need to get off my feet," Katie whispers to me.

"Me too." I wave to the crowd. "Alright y'all, it's time to go take a shower."

After a few more minutes of thanks and farewells, Katie and I hoist our packs into our respective vehicles. She rides with Kenny and I with Daniel. It's the first time in a week we aren't together, and her absence feels strange.

"Congratulations again," Daniel says.

"Thanks, that was pretty amazing." I sit in the passenger seat and look out the window at the passing trees and houses. My rugged body feels awkward sitting in such a clean and confined space. Nonetheless, sitting feels good. And having finished the thru-hike feels incomprehensible. *Did it really happen?* Of course it did. I can feel it in every muscle in my body. I can smell it on my sweat-crusted clothes and hair. The world flies by at forty-five miles per hour.

In twenty-five minutes, Daniel has driven the mileage Katie and I averaged each day. Back at the house, I hobble out of the car and set my pack on the front porch. Kenny pulls up and jumps out of the front seat.

"Katie's legs are pretty bad, so she's going to stay in the car," he explains.

I nod, helping him collect her things. It feels strange to be standing in my living room, in the same clothes I put on a week ago. I'm too tired to absorb the gravitas of the moment. All I want to do is shower, put on sweatpants, eat, and sleep.

"I think this is it," Kenny says, coming out of the kitchen with a bag of Katie's extra food she'd left behind.

"Yeah, I think so," I agree, surveying the room for any odds and ends.

"Way to go, lady. Get some rest." Kenny gives me a side hug with one arm.

"Thanks, Kenny. You too," I say. "And thanks for all you did supporting us and posting our updates." I limp out to their car.

Katie sits in the front seat, her legs stiff and swelling by the minute.

"Well, you're a true warrior," I say, leaning down.

"You too."

"Get home safely." I hug Katie again and give the hood a loving tap.

"We will." Kenny pulls away, driving south toward The Northway.

Outside my house, I stand on the sidewalk watching cars drive by. The sun lowers in the west and a few feather-like clouds drift across the blue September sky.

"Thank you," I whisper to the heavens, thinking of the angels around us and all the moments our nearly impossible mission seemed just that: impossible. Something bigger had pulled us through to this side.

I hobble to the bathroom and start the hot water. Sitting on the toilet lid, I prop my blistered toe onto my knee. With a pair of scissors, I slowly cut through the dirty layers of Leukotape and attempt to pull the tape from my toe, but it fiercely resists.

"Fine." I surrender and abandon my effort. Instead, I peel off my clothes and put the sweat-stained and dirty layers in the bathroom sink. Pine needles and flecks of dirt litter the floor. Naked, I step into the shower and steaming water cascades over my shoulders and down my legs. Water seeps into the tape as I wiggle my toes. More pine needles and twigs wash out from my tangled hair. With a loofah, I scrub my ankles and calves but let a few marks of earth stay. I'm not ready for the thru-hike to be completely washed from my skin.

The water drips to a stop, and I wrap a towel around my sore body and one around my hair. I sit once more and pull back the Leukotape. This time the grip releases.

"Ah, gross." I gag, quickly chucking the bloody, fleshy mess into the trash. The oozing, nickel-size hole is going to take a good amount of time to heal. Gently, I blot it with toilet paper. Using the heel of my foot, I limp to my bedroom and finally step into fresh underwear and sweats.

We did it, I text the group chat, even though word has spread quickly and everyone already knows Katie and I have finished. Setting my phone down, I glance at the time, before slipping under my quilt and curling up on my side. It's 6 p.m.

The Day After

September 18, 2020
0 miles
0 feet vertical gain

Coreys Road (1,740 ft.)

Fifteen hours later, I awake.

Warm September light has settled on the wooden panels of my bedroom floor. Outside, maple leaves flutter and blue jays call. I haven't moved from the position I fell asleep in. I gingerly bring my stiff feet to the floor. Against the hard surface, my toes do not fully flatten when I put weight on them. I waddle to the bathroom for a long overdue pee. Leaning hard on the bathroom sink, I push myself to a standing position.

In the kitchen, a fresh pot of coffee percolates and drips. I stretch my calves against the wall and drink some orange juice. Daniel's footsteps move across the floor upstairs, Tahawus's nails tick close behind.

When they reach the kitchen, he asks, "How'd you sleep?"

"Like the dead." I grab a bottle of extra-strength Tylenol from the cupboard. "How about you?" I ask, always worried about whether he has slept or not.

"I got some hours."

"That's good," I say. "Are you working from home today?"

"Yeah."

"Do you think you'll be able to get me out to pick up the

minivan, or should I try to find another ride?"

"I have time this afternoon," Daniel offers.

"Okay, cool. Thanks." I pour myself a steaming cup of coffee.

"Do you need anything for breakfast?"

"Nah, I think I'm going to make a bowl of leftovers," I say, knowing the refrigerator is full of food people brought to the finish yesterday. "Thanks though. Do you want any coffee?"

"Sure." He grabs a mug.

Gazing out the window, I see the birdhouse Daniel made when he was two weeks sober, one of the many distractions we explored in the early days. I remember it's his thirty-fourth birthday. A pang of guilt rushes over me.

"Oh, happy birthday! My brain's a little fuzzy this morning," I explain. But we both know the truth: He isn't the center of my world anymore.

"Thanks, and no worries."

We retreat to our respective levels of the house like polite roommates.

Back in my room, I sit on the bed, leaning against the headboard with two pillows propped under my legs. After hiking nearly two hundred miles in just over seven days, my body is finally still. It's an odd feeling, wondering what I'll do with so many hours in a day if I'm not moving. So, I sip on my coffee and flip open my computer. Maybe I'll write something. Maybe I should post something on the Instagram account I just figured out how to log in to. From my nightstand, I grab my phone and scroll through the photos I took during the thru-hike. The one of Katie and me standing in the MacIntyre Range and looking outward toward Allen Mountain on day three is my favorite.

I click on it and begin typing the Instagram caption:

Katie Rhodes and I just completed the 46 High Peaks in 7 days, 4 hours and 50 minutes unsupported. Meaning, we packed our packs, drove to one trailhead, climbed and camped our way through 64,000 feet of elevation and 180 miles. We had each other. To our knowledge we are the first women to do this.

The short post goes out to the few hundred people who follow my account. But when I flip over to Facebook, Katie and I are all over the main feed.

"Oh whoa." I blink and study the numbers. Kenny's daily reports have reached thousands upon thousands of people. No wonder we kept getting recognized on trail toward the end of our journey. Scrolling through the comments overwhelms me, so I set my computer aside. All I want to do is talk to Katie.

I text, *Hey chica! Hope you slept well. I did for fifteen hours, lol. Feeling pretty sore. How are your legs doing?*

Flexing my ankles, I roll them side to side and gaze out the window. Between my blistered toe, a thin, papery layer of skin has formed overnight. It's a miracle how quickly our bodies have the power to begin repairing themselves. Flooded with gratitude, I send Katie another, more lengthy text.

This feels like a dream to me. I just started looking at all the posts Kenny made each day and I'm so incredibly grateful for you. I wouldn't have been able to do this without you. I wouldn't have wanted to do it without you. You were the best partner I could have ever asked for. Thank you, Katie, you are amazing. And you are stronger than you even know.

After sending the message, I reply to a few congratulatory texts before powering down my phone and closing my eyes. I'll return to the modern world, but at my own pace. For now, I'll cling to the mountain vistas, like the dark Adirondack soil still clings to the backs of my ankles.

Later that afternoon, Daniel and I get ready to leave for Coreys Road. On the back porch, my empty pack and shoes are drying in the sun and a load of laundry churns upstairs. As I climb into the passenger seat of the car, a slender man bikes past me and pumps his fist.

"Woo-hoo Bethany! Yeah!" he yells.

It takes me a moment to register who it is. Jan. Like *the* Jan.

"Jan!" I call after him from the car window, waving enthusiastically. "Thank you!"

In seconds, he's down the road and out of sight. Holding onto the roof of the car, I think of the faded newspaper article tucked away in a wooden chest of keepsakes, between photos of family members and old birthday cards. Eleven years ago, two men I didn't know inspired me to do something that became a dedication, a mantra, a siren, something that fell away and called me back when I least expected it to. That mission was there when I desperately needed something to show me who I was and always had been, even in the foggiest and darkest of days. And now it is complete.

"Just think, you and Katie walked all of this," Daniel says as we drive past the trailhead for Cascade Mountain.

"Yeah, I don't think it's hit me quite yet," I respond, though yesterday morning already feels like a lifetime ago. In the passenger seat, I prop my bare feet on the dashboard and hang an arm out the open window. Hair blows across my face. An hour later, Daniel pulls in next to my minivan, which has been waiting patiently this whole time.

"Make sure it starts," he says.

"I will. I'm not walking home again," I joke.

Daniel smiles.

The minivan unlocks and I turn the key in the ignition. The engine turns over with no issue and I give Daniel a thumbs up. "All good."

"See you at the house." He waves before pulling out of the

parking lot.

"Uh, eww," I groan, noticing a line of mice turds on my dashboard. In the week it has been parked, my vehicle has been invaded. "Little bastards." I open my glove compartment. With a napkin, I push their dried droppings into the parking lot.

A beam of sunlight illuminates the trail register and I turn off my minivan. From the side door, I grab my grandmother's sweatshirt and throw it on, comforted by its familiar feel. I can't wait to visit and tell her about my journey. In a pair of flip-flops, I shuffle over to the beginning of it all. Opening the register box, I take the book in my hands and flip back to September 10, 2020. Even though fewer than a dozen groups of people have signed the pages in the days since, it seems like a lifetime ago. And maybe it was. Maybe that's what an adventure like this does to somebody. There's a lifetime of planning for it. Of trying for it, of crying for it, of pushing it away. Then there's the lifetime of doing it. And the lifetime that comes after it.

From the register I take the same half broken pencil with a flimsy piece of lead that I wrote with a week ago and add next to our entry, "Completed the unsupported thru-hike on 9/17. *We did it.*" With pride, I draw a star next to our entry and underline it twice. What we did is something to behold, celebrate, and share. And in this moment I finally have the courage to let go of all the things that came before and see what comes next.

Epilogue

ONE WEEK AFTER the thru-hike, I'm diagnosed with giardia and almost pass out from a high fever in front of a room full of students. Ironically, I had been talking about the thru-hike and water treatment. Apparently, water should be fully treated with iodine *before* Tailwind is added. Tailwind 2, Bethany 0.

Two weeks later, Governor Cuomo congratulates Katie and me for hiking all 46 High Peaks unsupported in his New York State Coronavirus Update email. Our section is appropriately titled, "Tonight's Deep Breath Moment."

Three weeks later, I return to the trail, setting another FKT in the Adirondacks on the Lake Placid 9er, a thirty-plus-mile route over nine smaller mountains. Now that my mind isn't so absorbed with the thru-hike, I realize how many FKT opportunities are out there and start scouting my next big one.

One month later, Daniel relapses, moves out of the house, and begins out-patient treatment. Our broken dam has fully released.

Ladened with grief and unable to get off the kitchen floor, I call Katie. She answers on the second ring and the sound of her voice brings me to tears.

"I feel like I can't breathe," I cry.

"Hey lady, it will be okay," she says. "You're stronger than you know."

I don't want to get up. But I do. And I don't want to go outside. But I grab Tahawus's leash and drive to the nearest trailhead, knowing the hardest climb is still before me. The only way through is to continue going back to the places that have healed me time and again. The mountains. My mountains.

46Climbs is an annual event that unites people in the fight against suicide. Through hiking and climbing mountains around the globe, participants raise life-saving funds for the American Foundation for Suicide Prevention (AFSP). The event aims to shift perceptions of mental health and suicide, fostering a culture of openness and support where those in crisis feel empowered to seek help. It also offers a meaningful opportunity to honor those we've lost and celebrate those still with us. Above all, 46Climbs serves as a powerful reminder that no one has to face their struggles alone.
—*Kolby T. Ziemendorf, cofounder of 46Climbs*

For more information about how you can join this community in the next 46Climbs event, visit 46Climbs.com. If you or someone you know is struggling, please reach out to the Suicide or Crisis Lifeline by texting or calling 988.

Gear List

Clothing and shoes:

La Sportiva Raptor trail running shoes

Three pairs of synthetic socks

One pair of lightweight pants

One polypro bottom set for sleeping

One lightweight long-sleeve synthetic shirt

One synthetic tank top

One sports bra

Two pairs of underwear

Set of rain shell and pants

One fleece top

One pair of sunglasses

One buff (a thin, tube-shaped piece of fabric worn around the head or neck)

One set of lightweight gloves

Pack and sleeping system:

45-liter REI Flash Pack

Ground pad (cut in half)

40-degree sleeping bag

Food and water system:

Bear canister (circular can with bear-safe locking system used to hold and protect food)

1.5 Liter water bottle

Iodine tablets (small pills used to purify water)

Shared gear:

Two-person tent

Stove, pot, and fuel (alcohol, 150 mL)

Lighter

Trekking poles

Emergency gear:

Cell phone

COVID-19 mask

Medical kit

Hygiene:

Seven baby wipes

Five maxi pads

Hand sanitizer

Toilet paper

Miscellaneous:

Headlamp (with fresh triple-A batteries, plus extra set of three batteries)

GPS watch

MP3 player

Day-by-Day Itinerary

Day 1: September 10

    Peaks: Seward, Donaldson, Emmons, Seymour (4) 4/46

    Miles: 21.6

    Elevation Gain: 7,380 feet

Day 2: September 11

    Peaks: Panther, Couchsachraga, Santanoni, Allen (4) 8/46

    Miles: 31.1

    Elevation Gain: 8,630 feet

Day 3: September 12

    Peaks: Marshall, Iroquois, Algonquin, Wright, Nye, Street, Phelps, Tabletop, Colden (9) 17/46

    Miles: 32.4

    Elevation Gain: 13,760 feet

Day 4: September 13*

    Peaks: Cliff, Redfield, Gray, Skylight, Marcy (5) 22/46

    Miles: 15

    Elevation Gain: 7,530 feet

Day 5: September 14*

Peaks: Haystack, Basin, Saddleback, Sawteeth, Gothics, Armstrong, Upper Wolf Jaw, Lower Wolf Jaw (8) 30/46

Miles: 14.7

Elevation Gain: 7,800 feet

Day 6: September 15

Peaks: Colvin, Blake, Nippletop, Dial, Dix, Hough, South Dix, Macomb, Grace (9) 39/46

Miles: 17.8

Elevation Gain: 9,100 feet

Day 7: September 16

Peaks: Giant, Rocky Peak Ridge, Big Slide, Porter, Cascade (5) 44/46

Miles: 29.4

Elevation Gain: 11,000 feet

Day 8: September 17

Peaks: Whiteface and Esther (2) 46/46

Miles: 21.2

Elevation Gain: 4,400 feet

Originally, before the storm, Days 4 and 5 were going to be combined.

Totals: 7 days, 4 hours, 50 minutes

Peaks: 46

Miles: 183.2

Elevation Gain: 69,600

Acknowledgements

My parents, you were there for it all.

My sisters, you inspire me.

Maegan Dills, for encouraging me to climb my first High Peak.

Cory and Jan, you did the impossible and planted a seed.

Tim Horvath, my mountain mentor and hyperlight guru.

Katie, for reaching out on a rainy day when my soul needed an expedition and a friend. I will always be grateful to you for that September week in the High Peaks.

Jason Pageau, for your colorful soul and inspiration.

Marin George, for giving me light on the darkest days.

To every soul I've shared trail miles with.

Mrs. Thienpont, my middle school English teacher who told me I'd be a writer, even when English was my least favorite subject.

To all my teachers in college, who showed me writing was more than punctuation. It was storytelling.

Carl Lennertz, who opened the door on how to write a book.

Katie Ives, who encouraged me to keep pursuing publishers.

Christine Reed, who saw what this could be. *Unsupported* would not be here without you and your talent to share stories. Thank you for the countless hours you poured into this book.

Jessica Hill and Jen Swanson, for pulling out and putting together the missing details and extending deadlines. I'm entirely grateful to you.

Sarah Kulfan and Megan Vickery, for a beautiful cover that captures the spirit of the High Peaks.

Jon Winslow, for lugging expensive cameras up steep mountains to get the most magnificent shots.

Tahawus, you are the best co-writer and snuggle support system.

Adrian, who expanded my faith and led me on a path of healing. It has been your love and support that got me writing again. You are my here and now.

And to the sandy soils and blue ridges of the Adirondack Mountains, this is all because of you.

A Note from the Author

When I first heard about the unsupported thru-hike in 2009, I went to The Mountaineer gear shop, in Keene Valley, in search of a book on it. Surely, there would be something about FKTs in the Adirondacks. There wasn't. Young and idealistic, I didn't realize how niche the sport of FKTs were, but I did meet Jan Wellford, one of the current record holders, that day.

Life is all about those interactions, brief moments with a certain person or idea that end up having a profound impact on your very own purpose and trajectory. I cannot thank the Adirondack Mountains enough for the healing and the home they have provided me since 2009.

Fifteen years in the making, I have done my best to honor this story. And there were many times I thought it would never make it to print. From the failed attempts in 2012 and 2016, to the personal breakdown of my marriage in 2020, it was not how I envisioned it to be. But what ever is? In the end, this story is more raw and true. And because of that all the more important to share.

Please remember that this story is told through my perspective. Certain names, events, and conversations have been changed to help honor the privacy of others. However when it comes to the specific details of the unsupported thru-hike, I have done my best to accurately represent what Katie and I did, by going through trip reports we wrote, and presentations we gave after our accomplishment in 2020.